Three Came Home from the Woods

Three Came Home from the Woods
A Memoir of the Mind's Eye

Rohn Federbush

CHB Media, Publisher

Copyright 2023 © Rohn Federbush

All Rights Reserved
including the right of reproduction,
copying, or storage in any form
or means, including electronic,
in whole or part,
without prior written
permission of the author.

ISBN 979-8-9873184-1-6
LIBRARY OF CONGRESS CONTROL NUMBER: 2023935157

CHB MEDIA, PUBLISHER

(386) 492-6568

chbmedia@gmail.com
www.chbbooks.com

First Edition
Printed in the USA

FOREWORD

WHAT KIND OF STORY IS *Three Came Home from the Woods*? Is it truly a story about Dissociative Identity Disorder (DID), formerly known as Multiple Personality Disorder, in the manner of *Three Faces of Eve* or *Sybil*? Or is it a contemporary allegory in which a woman coming of age in the 1960s is whipsawed between traditional and newly possible feminine roles and develops divergent personalities to cope will all that's demanded of her? Can we know for sure? And how clear is the line that separates the two?

In her Preface author Rohn Federbush seems to suggest the latter is the case, but she sets her three "identities," her three "personalities," in the office of a therapist whose clear mission is to find a portal through which the three will step to emerge as one. She has left us, her readers, with a bit of a mystery to unravel, which is part of the fun of *Three Came Home from the Woods*.

One thing we know for sure is that ninety percent of people afflicted with Dissociative Identity Disorder are women. Ms. Federbush shows remarkable vision in describing a woman's perception of that cusp between the 1950s and the 60s, when feminist horizons were expanding but obligations of wife, mother, daughter, and homemaker were bound as tightly as ever.

In a nod to the importance of place in storytelling, she toggles back and forth between conservative Midwestern towns and the city of Ann Arbor, effectively capturing the billowing atmosphere of this liberal oasis, home of the University of Michigan, the "Hash Bash," and the Rainbow People's Party.

"Wait a minute," one might say as they delve into

the story, "Aren't people who have DID usually unaware of the existence of the other identities?" In Ms. Federbush's story, the three "personalities" seem to know each other quite well. It's true, that ignorance of the others was considered to be a DID requirement until just recently. In stories like *Eve* or *Sybil* it takes deep therapy to ferret out what is happening. And that therapy is only initiated after a husband or some other person reports that the DID patient appears to be different people at different times, with the various identities called forth to cope with situations they are better equipped to handle.

Until the most recent edition, the *Diagnostic and Statistical Manual of Mental Disorders* (DSM) required that the signs and symptoms had to be observed by others. But one important change from the fourth to the fifth edition of the DSM is that individuals may now report their perception of personality shifts rather than limiting diagnosis to shifts reported by others.

I am not a psychiatric professional, so I won't offer a definitive opinion on whether *Three Came Home from the Woods* is a true multiple personalities tale or an allegory of one woman's fight for her own identity. I will leave that to you, the reader. As you read, pay special attention to the divergent pronouns used by the three identities to describe themselves: Nancy refers to herself in the second person "you." Betty employs the third person plural, "they" or "them." Sara calls herself "I." These variations are a useful literary device, but they also are important to the arc of the story.

—Gary Broughman
Executive Editor, CHB Media

Preface

TRAUMATIC EVENTS in the average woman's life create different personalities to deal with each stage. Marriage dreams can turn into lonesome divorce realities that cry out for happy endings. This creative non-fiction tale follows my eight-decade path. One healing fictional séance meshes the three disjointed roles into one functioning, transformed woman.

The marriage ordeals of a young mother propel her to abandon herself. Her radical feminist takeover personality ends up a chaotic divorcee who uses men and alcohol to ameliorate her suffering. After fifty years of failing to subdue their demons, the multiple personalities seek relief through the services of a psychologist who promises to keep them together in a happy-ever-after life. My husband gave me the ending when the hero-doctor uses the *Man of La Mancha* ending, pulling out a mirror for the three to see they are one, a *Three Faces of Eve* redemption story that most women experience.

—Rohn Federbush

PROLOGUE
RICK FITZGERALD

Winter, Big Wolf Lake, Michigan

RICK FITZGERALD FLATTENED his hand against the cold windowpane. He wished the Michigan sky could stay half as blue as the potted hydrangeas at the foot of each window. The icy sheen on Big Wolf Lake's snow-covered surface reflected the dwindling winter sun.

Near the lake's center the last patch to freeze held less snow. A cross-country skier headed toward the dangerous circle. Realizing his error, the outdoorsman headed back to the shore's safer territory.

Rick turned away to survey the tea cart his wife Tanya had prepared for at least a half-dozen guests. No one would go away hungry if she had anything to do about it. After sampling one of her raisin tarts, he thanked the Lord for his home, his faith, and the opportunity to listen to new clients. Tanya had referred the three personalities about to descend on him. She'd convinced Rick to turn a séance into a constructive therapy session for the woman.

Tanya explained he could easily differentiate the women by their use of different pronouns. Sara used the first person "I"; Nancy referred to herself as "you" while she consistently tapped her chest in a "mia-culpa" gesture, and Betty used the plurals (they, their, and them). Tanya's last words of guidance were, "Don't forget to ask them how politics in the Sixties revolutionized their thinking."

Rick promised half-heartedly, "I'm willing to try."

A talent for creating enough mystery around calming meditation techniques gained him a reputation for effective séances. Without qualms Rick availed himself of every means necessary to turn misery into joy-filled lives. So what if the terminology of his tactics didn't coincide with the professional lexicon of certified psychologists. His intentions were commendable.

Convinced the other side of reality held depths of wisdom in an unconscious pool of the departeds' memories, Rick delved into the farthest expanses of the universe. Augmented by the prods of relatives' voices, seekers absorbed new insights. If a patient had admired or respected their lost tutors enough, Rick's suggestions extricated lingering and harmful emotions. He didn't fear inserting his knowledge of saints and philosophers long-gone to aid in the process—what was heaven for if not to enlighten those left behind?

Above his head the pink glass dome with its purple sunburst and violet frame let in all the light left in the day. As the grandfather clock struck four, Tanya opened the door for his new clients to assemble.

From a stooped position Nancy Peach swung her heavy red-and-white checkered cape off her shoulders, barely missing the Tiffany vase on its stand next to the door. As Rick reached for the vase and caught her coat, Nancy said, "Sorry," then swept her long dark-brown hair back, tucking it behind her ears. "Artists aren't very neat guests, are you?" she said with her characteristic chest tapping.

"You're fine, Nancy," Tanya said as she left the room.

"How are the boys, young men, I mean?" Rick said, "I'm glad you came."

* * *

Nancy Peach

"They're both well, you'd think." Nancy diminished as she took in her surroundings. The circular room's rainbow-colored furnishing swirled around her. To stop her dizziness she concentrated on the glass dome above her, and then asked, "Leave the entrance open just a bit?" In the catholic gesture of repentance, Nancy's closed fist hit her chest. "You often sense being caged."

Was this guy a real clairvoyant? His athletic body hinted he was fit from running or some equally horrendous activity. His blue eyes and tousled, light-brown hair were more appropriate for a poet than a doctor of psychology. Would the blue velvet drapes be pulled shut for the reading? Nancy planned to feel under the coffee table for wires if anything unusual happened. Surely answers from the dead were impossible to predict. Nevertheless, she wanted desperately to ask Mother if she was talented enough to join Ann Arbor's artist group, even if Sara and Betty discouraged her.

As a young girl in St. Charles, Illinois, Nancy studied figure drawing from library books. Mother had been pleased when Nancy sketched her, erasing all signs of age. Encouraged, Nancy took her new skills to work and drew the faces of fellow secretaries.

In 1994 Nancy hadn't enough time away from the demands of her university job to say a proper goodbye to

Mother. In the back bedroom of the Florida mobile home, Mother raised her right arm in goodbye. On the phone the last week of her life, Nancy fed Mother religion's pabulum, "Angels will lift you up to heaven." And on the last day's phone call Nancy's oldest niece described Mother flapping her arms. As Nancy predicted, Mother experienced her ascent with the promised angels.

Rick's voice meddled with Nancy's thoughts. "I'd like to hear how political changes during the Sixties impacted all your lives."

Nancy tasted her left index finger. "You were twenty-three when Cronkite's summary of President Kennedy's assassination interrupted your soap. You were living in an Elgin upstairs apartment with your husband and son. Johnny was at work. Carl was playing on the scatter rug in front of the television. You swept him into your arms and rushed downstairs to see if your younger neighbor had watched the terrible news. You remember saying, 'You didn't vote for the man, but they can't just murder your President.' You guess you're still aren't sure who the 'they' were. On the way home from church, you heard about Oswald's execution in the jail's entrance hall—of all places."

Nancy sat on Rick's dark green couch and drifted away. She could hear Betty Pozner butting into the topic under consideration.

"We never fit our husband John's standards for a wife." Betty bit her lip. "John told us Kennedy deserved to be killed. How did we decide to marry such a crude creature?"

Nancy welcomed the calmer response she heard from Sara Powell, "John looked like a great white hunter, lined square face, bulky shoulders." Sara rubbed her chin. "At six-foot-five he seemed a worthy candidate to father healthy children. Both my sisters had babies by the time I married at twenty."

Nancy regained their attention. "Mother and Daddy brought you to Blue Moon dances in St. Charles when you were nineteen. Marrying you off was their goal. They already thought you were an old maid."

Sara added, "Mine were not happy when I asked for a desk and a typewriter instead of the hope chests both of my sisters had assembled. Rather competitive, they both married in the same year. Etta the oldest was nineteen." Sara touched the tip of her nose. "She had three miscarriages before giving birth to a baby girl, who lived for a day. That was 1956 before premature medicine had made such great strides." Sara stroked her face with both hands, keeping their attention locked on her next words. "My sophomore biology classmates were too cheerful. How could the world continue without noting a child's passing? My first poem memorialized her short life. I haven't stopped writing since. Jean married at seventeen. Nine months later her daughter Cindy was Mother's first grandchild."

Rick stopped Sara's recitation of family history. "How did the assassinations affect you?"

Sara was silenced for a second.

Since Nancy already had her say, she hoped Betty would keep quiet until Sara formulated an answer.

Sara finally said, "So many books have been written about Kennedy. One of the surprises for me was the blatant immorality of the entire family. From then on, the media felt they had a license for muckraking, revealing more about public figures than we ever wanted to know. Leaders should inspire young people, not teach them how to cheat and lie."

Betty couldn't shut up any longer. "After those exposés, society took its pleasures wherever and whenever they wanted. The birth control pill came out about the same time. You can see why we'll never run for public office, can't you?"

"Right." Nancy laughed. "You wouldn't want your children answering questions about how they survived all those—meetings."

"We kept our love-life out of the children's sight." Betty lifted her chin as if anticipating a blow. "Do they complain about us?"

Sara coughed. "They saw the numbers arriving to escort you. And their wives recycled your history to badger both Carl and Tom."

Nancy lowered her head. She wanted to remember why she had come. All these societal transformations didn't interest her. When had she started to believe she could paint? She was still living at home when she took an art test in some magazine. After she sent in a naked sketch of herself draped in Mother's quilt, the questionable mail-order school wanted her to pay for long-distance classes.

Instead, Nancy had commandeered one of her house-painting father's unused rolls of wallpaper to lay out a Chinese scene on its backside. Misty mountains, shaded pagodas and lounging costumed figures graced the three-by-six foot mural. Her middle sister, Jean, asked to have it framed, which Daddy did. Jean hung the painting in the living room of her first home. The scarcity of a furniture budget provided the room with a black-painted round table with its legs cut off, a fake drawered red-and-black credenza and giant red cushions. When Jean moved to California, Etta, the oldest sister, was awarded the painting. Nine years later Nancy found the mural in Etta's basement recreation room still framed but damaged by a fallen lamp's attack.

One high-school summer when Nancy worked as a pediatricians' receptionist, a nurse in the practice asked for a mural too. Nancy drove to Naperville on weekends to paint a troop of fun-loving clowns to decorate the walls of basement steps to a recreation room.

After Nancy married Johnny, a friend from DuKane, the electronics firm in St. Charles, commissioned a Chinese mural, too. He'd provided a long strip of Mylar. Very pregnant, Nancy developed an allergy to the acrylic paints, but finished her first paid assignment.

She attempted a further answer to Rick's political question. "Before they shot the president, the media brought similar appalling bulletins." In 1962, Nancy had just finished reading Look magazine's article with the picture layout of Marilyn Monroe's visit to Carl Sandburg. When the media broadcast Marilyn had committed suicide, there was a connection in Nancy's mind to an earlier scene.

When she was pregnant with Carl in 1961 in their Elgin apartment, one of Johnny's acquaintances visited. Even though the story had nothing to do with being an artist, Nancy thought the psychologist would want to know. "A young man, who had been Johnny's boarding-house roommate, wouldn't speak to you or even acknowledge your presence in the room. When the boy returned home to St. Charles, he hung himself. He must have loved your husband. When he saw how pregnant you were, he grew despondent. Marilyn Monroe loved someone who rejected her, too. She couldn't acknowledge any hope beyond her pain." Nancy guessed the young man couldn't either. "You can't even remember his name. He was your height, underdeveloped compared to big, strapping Johnny."

"You were Roman Catholic before you married?" Rick asked.

"Yes and they believed people who commit suicide go to hell. You suppose Baptists still believe that. Johnny was a Bible Fundamentalist."

"Back then, no one accepted bisexuals in society, do they now?" Betty always had the last word.

Nancy understood it was just to gain their attention—usually by adding a question—but she wanted Rick to answer her, not Betty.

Rick said, "Men of questionable predilections often needed marriage to become acceptable enough for employment."

Nancy wound a strand of hair around her finger. "Your heart in 2017 was just more indulgent of sexual predispositions."

Again, Betty had to comment, "Wives suffered tremendously because of the lack of passion and any real love from our husbands, didn't we?"

"We certainly hear more about bisexuals now," Sara concluded. "When I was eighteen, Mother asked me what homosexuals did when they made love. I'd read enough novels off the Catholic sanctioned list to precisely describe their actions."

Rick seemed determined to keep them on track. "Did you take note of any other social upheavals outside your family?"

But Nancy wanted to focus on the more soothing subject of her painting history. Around 1963 when both boys were down for their naps, Nancy attempted to make watercolors of several encyclopedia pictures of Roman ruins. The South Elgin kitchen table in their first house provided ready access to water and the necessary clean-up.

Unannounced, Etta and Mother knocked on the kitchen door for a visit. By the time they left, the children were up. Those paintings were never finished.

At twenty-five Nancy moved to Ann Arbor with her husband for his four-state traveling job. He managed to come home every other weekend. Her time was finally her own except for the boys. She'd made several sketches of the children and one oil painting of her three-year-old struggling to wash his hands in the bathroom sink.

She paused on that happy note, admitting to Rick, "Your safe world evaporated in 1965. The bloodshed of the Viet Nam War was brought into your living room. Bombings, bodies, and bleeding soldiers overshadowed the evening reports." Nancy shook her head, trying to dislodge the painful images.

"Did Martin Luther King's death or Robert Kennedy's in early 1968 influence you?" Rick asked.

"Who could remain a stone after the Democratic Convention police riots that year?" Betty strident question filled the room. "We became Democrats. John remained a Republican. Did serving in the Navy cause his wooden heart?"

Nancy went back to twirling the strand of hair near her left ear. "You know your eldest boy, Carl, enlisted in the service and spent nine years in submarines. They just produced one more polite, cold-hearted Republican."

Sara admitted, "I started smoking Virginia Slims in 1968. Their advertising slogan, 'We've come a long way, baby,' resonated with me. African-Americans fought for their equality, but they raised awareness for women, too."

"Was it the pill or feminism that made us feel sexually equal to men?" Betty asked.

"But not as smart," Nancy said.

"Isn't that another complete story of yours, Sara?" Betty laughed that irritating laugh of hers.

Returning to her less contentious ruminations, Nancy reminisced about her Illinois divorce in 1969. "After two brief reconciliations, Johnny left you. He moved in with a young man."

When Betty became involved with a beautiful Italian bartender, Nancy drew a life-size pencil sketch of the reclining nude on the wall next to Betty's bed. After she ended the relationship, the Italian broke into Betty's Federal-housing apartment. Nancy could barely remember the chaotic details. Had Betty swallowed all the birth-control pills in the medicine cabinet? Nancy did recall Betty kneeling besides the boys' beds. They were understandably terrified. Hospitalized for one night after her stomach was pumped, Betty was referred to her first therapist.

Jean, their middle sister, insisted they all stay with her, but Betty took advantage of her hospitality for just one night. They were determined to survive on their own.

The art class Jean insisted on paying for let Nancy produce a beautiful long-stem red rose, a water color of an abandoned barn and several Gibson styled portraits of picturesque women.

Nancy breathed in deeply, relishing her successful endeavors. "You did drag the boys to protests against the Viet Nam war. One cold evening in 1973, you stood on the sidewalk below Elgin's Tower building with the snow floating down around you."

"Sara can tell you about her protests in Jackson, Michigan early in 1969, too." Betty refocused Rick's interest by asking, "After Nixon resigned, why didn't Liberals celebrate getting rid of a President and stopping the war?"

Nancy's single life as a painter was stifled even after

both boys started their own lives. However after Sara married Powell in 1990, his Aunt Claire paid for her life-time membership in the Ann Arbor City Club. Nancy painted with a group of artists at the club every Friday.

She attempted watercolors but settled on oil paints as the easiest medium to manipulate. Not a craft-maker or seamstress, Nancy's family and friends were showered instead with paintings. There were not enough walls in Sara's condo to hang Nancy's rapid production. Come spring, Nancy planned to cover the walls in the garage with the unframed oils.

Her younger brother, Lee, deemed one still-life worthy enough to hang in his front room where the setting sun shone on the cobalt-blue subjects making them sparkle as if they were real glass. However when Nancy attempted a portrait of Lincoln—Lee was after all a lawyer and born in Illinois—he said it resembled perhaps a cousin of Lincoln's.

The City Club hung several of her paintings temporarily, but Nancy wasn't sure of what price to ask. Giving them away didn't require monetary evaluations. She wondered how Rick could hope to help her—or Betty, and Sara.

This psychologist, Rick, didn't even know the history of her birthing parents, or the traumas that defined Betty's aggression, Sara's strength, or her own need for recognition. She pulled her skirt up a little and crossed her shapely legs, hoping Rick would appreciate the last remnants of her youth. Betty told Nancy legs were the last to go.

CHAPTER ONE
FARM IN MCLEAN COUNTY, ILLINOIS
1928

ETTA NORTH PEACH turned the yellowing photograph toward the window. Try as she might, she failed to match the unsmiling cross-armed woman with feet planted in front of a small log cabin with her energetic fun-loving mother. She slid the corner of the photo into the mirror's frame and tiredly put away her mourning clothes. She'd outlived her father, brothers and sisters, and now her mother had passed.

After donning her house dress, Etta—Nancy's grandmother and her sister's namesake—wrapped the apron around her slim waist and went through the small parlor with its table of dried roses under a glass bowl to the unused dining room and into the kitchen. She could smell the meaty aroma of the roast-goose supper she had started in the morning. She was stirring the gravy when Israel came in from the barn. He hadn't gone to the funeral. It was a relief that her minister had picked her up. Etta didn't need to watch her stockings the way she did when Israel spit tobacco into the rusted coffee can next to the gearshift.

She carefully poured gravy into her mother's white gravy dish as Israel came up behind her. She could smell the barn. Sometimes Etta ignored the reek if she wanted sex bad enough—as their brood of nine kids proved. He kissed the back of her neck, but she shook him off. "Call the kids. None of them has set the table."

"Was there a large turnout?"

"No. Most of her friends died long ago."

Nine children, from the ages of twenty-one to three, trouped in and sat down on the long benches. Etta went to the cupboard, pulled out a stack of dishes and threw them at the door. That got their attention. She ran back to the bedroom, half in fear of Israel's ready slaps—but mostly just to be alone.

* * *

Israel should have gone to the funeral, but the cow might have calved while he was away. "You kids clean up that mess and quit crying," he said, "or I'll give you something to cry about."

Vernita his eldest daughter went to the cupboard to find more plates but there were none. Etta did break dishes on occasion, but the broken ones on the floor seemed to be the last of them.

A redhead, Etta had been the prize in the county in their courting days. His mother was shocked when he brought home this fiery lanky girl, a head taller than he.

Directing the children to the stove, Israel said. "Take turns now. You older ones feed the little ones so they don't get burnt." He left them bellied up to the stove with goose-meat in their fingers, forks playing with the mashed potatoes or corn. They looked like animals around a feeding trough.

He took one goose leg from the hand of Jessie, his buck-toothed daughter, and cautiously approached Etta still holed up in their bedroom. He didn't mind her temper.

His was worse. He figured they were both high-spirited. Their bed scenes were always a storm.

Three years ago, after she announced she was with child, Israel had gotten pretty drunk. He'd come home roaring, revving up his junker. He refused to get out of the old Ford, screaming he was going to kill himself. The younger kids were yelling and clinging to her skirts or each other. She'd calmed the little ones down and took everyone back into the house. With no audience, Israel quieted down too.

He had sheepishly slid into their bed with his clothes still on.

She undressed him against his protests. "I'm already pregnant. Now let's enjoy it."

They had a great time, the alcohol a further spur for their normal passion for each other. He knew she had Indian blood. His mother had been adamant, trying to deter him from marrying so early. In fact the homestead belonged to the Norths in the Shawnee tribe more than a hundred years before Israel's family arrived from the east at the beginning of the Civil War.

But Israel had arrived with other dreams—of glass-domed gardens and red velvet chairs on pretty blue carpets. The land didn't draw him to its embrace. The animals never multiplied fast enough and the weather was out of his control. He wanted to stay young, to dance to his heart's content with flirty women and to hear music all day long.

He blamed his father for his ill fit as a farmer. His father's name, Orlando Israel Peach, could be traced back to a Massachusetts militia man in the Revolutionary War. The family carried the name for second sons, reversing the first two names each generation. Most wars took the first born, so the second male preserved the family name down to Udale's brother, Orlando Israel.

* * *

The oldest boy, Udale (Nancy's father), was the main target of his own father's frustration. Once when Israel was digging a new hole for the outhouse, nine-year-old Udale decided to watch. Israel didn't enjoy an audience for the menial task. He saw himself on a higher plane, classier. He threw a shovel of dirt at his son.

Udale thought it an accident and moved to the other side of the hole. Israel tossed another shovel-full at him. Udale didn't move. He stared into his father's eyes not wanting to believe the anger and hatred.

Even when he tried to please, Udale faced a hopeless task. He graduated from eighth grade but not before Israel came into the one-room school to drag Udale out to help with the spring harvest of winter wheat.

One of Udale's first real jobs on a neighboring farm included brushing the horses. His new boss yelled at him, "Now how ya goin get rid of the dirt that a-way? Brush against the hair, then you can get the dust up."

When Nancy's daddy, Udale, told her about the incident, he called it the "more than one right way to do a job" story.

Udale tried his new skill at home, but Israel grabbed the iron-toothed brush and scrapped it over his son's head, twice. "How does that feel? Don't hurt the damn beast, just brush the dirt out!"

* * *

In 1948 after Daddy lost another farm-managing job, Mother broke her pelvis—falling or jumping from a haymow. Daddy drove his daughters down to his mother's farm in Illinois while he looked for work. Nancy, the youngest of the three, followed her paternal grandmother's every step. One cool morning when a breeze kept the constant flies at bay, Grandma (North) Peach called the sole child in the yard to her side.

Nancy rarely gained favor. Her oldest sister, Etta, named for this grandmother, was the prettiest—blonde and vain, while Jean possessed a sweet helpful disposition. Grandma Peach had just cut the throat of a rooster and was washing it under the pump. She showed Nancy how to hold the craw to make the sound of a rooster by blowing through it—a savage thing to teach a child. Nancy could imagine the revenging Shawnee creeping over the flat fields with the dawn, throating out the faked rooster's crow to slay the settlers still secure in their warm cabin beds.

When Nancy was fourteen in 1954 well versed in the rights of women, this widowed grandmother held court, arguing the ills of the world were due to women voting. Mother directed Nancy to leave the room. Nancy walked off her rage before being allowed to rejoin polite company.

When Grandma Peach's mind started to bend with age, she shared the secrets which might have been lost in the eternal fog. There was Shawnee blood in the family. She called her own mother a squaw. Did the Shawnee teach grandma how to mimic a rooster's crow? Daddy's black thick hair and high cheek bones could be the legacy. Marriage and Christianity wiped out nearly all traces of race, names, language, and heritage.

Divorce was not a financial option back then, but the suffering took its toll on the nine Peach children. Three died of complications from ulcers, two from hyper-tension strokes, which started when they were emotionally abused. Even though the corporal punishment wasn't constant, nowadays the courts would have intervened on the children's behalf.

Nancy's father, Udale, died—ulcer ridden and stroke-racked, angry at the world, and ruing life's bitter end. He could find his voice when sufficiently provoked. Six months before he died, he threw a bowl of tomato soup at his nursing home roommate for changing the television channel without his permission.

* * *

On Nancy's mother's side, her grandfather at four foot-eleven had enough gumption to sire eleven handsome children, the type others stop to stare after. He retired as a switchman on the railroad. He'd also used his carpentry skills for the inside of cabooses. Grandpa Kerner drank and beat his children. Once, Mother drained a year's supply of fermenting wine kept in the basement.

His parents lived a block away on the other side of their grape-arbor. Great-grandfather Kerner, a tall elegant man with a graying mustache, wasn't Grandpa's real father. Nancy found out from her aunts after her mother, Marie, died that Great-grandmother Kerner had been pregnant when Great-grandfather married her. The two didn't look like father and son at all. Grandpa was short and mean. Of the other three children, younger than Grandpa, one became a Bishop, one a nun, and the other an old maid. None was as fecund as Grandpa Simon Kerner.

Grandma Kerner, a Marksteiner, was fourteen when she arrived in America from St. Anne, Hungary. She worked as a maid and cook until she married at sixteen. Grandma had those eyes that could pin the hurt down and pluck it out just by the business of living. She died at age one hundred and two. Within a year five of her daughters followed her path to the other side.

* * *

Nancy's daddy courted this Bloomington city gal on

horseback as often as he could. Mother saw him as an escape. However, she was fired from her secretarial job when she announced the wedding. She hadn't expected to learn how inconvenient outside plumbing could be. At least, she never allowed her children to watch the farm animals mate.

That summer in 1948 when Nancy and Jean left Grandma Peach's idle household, Grandma Kerner took them into her Bloomington home. When Nancy's mother healed sufficiently from her fall from the haymow, she visited Grandma Kerner with Nancy's younger brother, Lee. Lee called Nancy "Me" and himself "Dee." Lee tried to take away a pair of scissors Grandma had given Nancy. They made quite a racket. Mother came out and pulled on Nancy's hair until she relinquished the scissors to give Lee a turn. As the third daughter with a favored younger brother, Nancy learned to expect last place in anyone's affection.

Actually Nancy's mother should have been a nun. She lived with her high-German paternal grandmother from the age of two until she was nine. Lying perfectly still for years in her maiden aunt's Catholic bed was motivation enough to walk back across the grape arbor and refuse to leave her mother's house. Considered an outsider from the other ten siblings, that fact didn't instill a loving heart in Mother. She knew all the words, but her tone of sincerity lacked believable warmth—for Nancy.

CHAPTER TWO
RICK FITZGERALD

RICK INTERRUPTED NANCY'S family musings by offering Betty a cup of freshly poured tea. His dismissive appraisal of Nancy's sexual ploy conformed to his early training in psychology. Her use of the pronoun "you," made her conversation complicated—if it hadn't been for the habitual chest rap clue. But Rick decided it was Nancy's way of acknowledging she was part of a multiple personality—just as Betty chose "we." But did Nancy know her own motivations were plainly evident, or would he determine her innocence in the tactic? She did hunch forward, rarely making eye contact with him. Perhaps she didn't understand what she was telegraphing by raising her skirt and crossing her well-formed legs. Rick hoped he could establish enough trust for her to share her impulses without undue prodding. Nancy's definition of an artist might include the belief that creative freedom was based on loose morals released from the confines of musical scales or the edges of sketch pads.

Betty had tugged off her red boots and wooly socks, replacing them with shoes which matched her herringbone suit. Straightening and throwing her shoulders back, she held Rick's gaze and asked, "What does a professional therapist think of our favorite color?"

"Did the Wellingtons come with the socks?" Rick asked.

"You're good. You answer all questions with a question, don't you?" She sipped the peach tea when he didn't answer.

Rick scratched the back of his leg with the toes of his other foot.

As if noticing the black tips of his socks, Betty asked, "Should we take off our shoes?"

"I can answer that." Rick laughed. "No, your shoes are fine. The floor does have a bit of a draft this time of year."

Sara Powell had wrapped her long hair into an intricate knot with the help of a red barrette. As she unwound her red scarf and placed the matching gloves on the neatly folded scarf, Sara answered Betty's question, "Yoga masters say the red life-blood at the seat of the body heats the flow in our veins for sexual arousal. Mr. Fitzgerald, is that why you've carpeted this lovely room in red?"

"Meditation techniques are always of value," Rick said. He pointed to the orange pillows. "The colors are unusual, but I don't think the tones clash. Orange is the color of burning resentments, the yellow walls promise we can be our real joyful selves, the green couch is the color of affection, and the blue drapes the breath of life." He pointed to the dome above them. "Violet and purple symbolize the soul's communion with our Creator."

"You don't think those shades wrestle with each other," Nancy said. "You love producing something pleasing to the eye. Painting from black and white photographs, you insert Gauguin's bright choices. He just understood people respond to primary colors. Your wife beautified this room? It's a cheery place for a winter's brunch."

"Might be the yellow walls," Sara said.

Betty pushed her aside. "Rick, why didn't you arrange the séance stage with drawn black drapes and flickering candles?"

"True mystics don't need all of the standard paraphernalia." Rick had motioned for them to enjoy their tea.

Before she sat down, Sara had stroked the side of the white glass pot-bellied stove as if to warm her hands. "How can you tell which book you're reaching for?" She gestured toward the low bookshelves around the room, sporting light blue covers on all their occupants.

"A good memory." Rick laughed. "Or maybe I like to test my psychic powers. Tanya and I visited the Long Room in Dublin's library. The three-floor-high stacks of books were each covered with light-brown paper. Tanya said book covers would make this room too busy." Rick poured himself a cup of tea. "Now each of you explain why you came."

In the quiet that followed, Sara raised her head. "I don't know why I'm here. Except at times I feel like I'm spaced out—as if I'm not even real. I wanted to listen to what you tell them. Sometimes when Nancy or Betty arrives and I'm with friends it's humiliating. I can't control the way they speak or act. And the friends they bring along are even worse!" Sara wrapped her arms around herself, before saying, "You may be a writer yourself, Rick, under the delusion your imagination brings you messages from the other side when you are really a novelist, like me. I think I daydream, I mean write fiction, to distract myself from feeling lonely. I love peopling my world."

Rick shook his head. "It's amazing to me how writers string out a plot and make characters come alive. How many novels have you finished?"

"All of them," Sara said. "I've self-published a dozen, but five others are completed."

"You'll never give up, will you?" Betty patted Sara's knee as if to reassure her comrade. "Rick, will you provide more insight than the string of therapists we've richly compensated throughout the years?"

Nancy spoke next. "Please just ask Mother if she knew you were gifted. You think you might have more confidence. You wonder if your ability is inherited. Daddy was a house painter after he gave up farming. He attempted oil paintings once he'd retired to Florida. You tried encouraging your boys, but neither of them seemed interested in such endeavors. Your youngest enjoys being his own house painter, if that amounts to anything."

Betty laughed. "Proud to say, never changed a diaper."

"Betty is a goddess in your estimation," Nancy said, stroking her chest with her fist. "You enjoy being a good mother. Women who play at housekeeping are worthless. You're a homemaker. A friend revealed you would climb lofty buildings for your boys. Maybe you should have pushed your ideals on them more. You just hoped they would build their own moral compasses. You should have had more children. As it was Johnny bragged about being the only one of his five brothers, to produce two males in a row. But Tom was nine pounds fifteen ounces and you birthed him naturally. If you pick up a ten pound bag of potatoes imagine you giving birth. When they said you had a boy, you kept saying you knew and you were happy, having a girl. The nurses would repeat the word *boy*, but your mind wouldn't accept it, so you repeated for them you knew you had a *girl*.

"After the birth they put you in a room with three other new mothers. We were all chatting away. We might have been making too much noise laughing. A huge frowning nurse burst in and yelled at us. We were supposed to be resting. Your spirits plummeted. When the same nurse brought Tom to you, you said he wasn't yours, refusing to hold him.

"Tom was bright red and his black hair hung to his shoulders. Your first son, Carl, had been a blue eyed, blond perfect little baby. They whisked you off to a private room. When your physician arrived, he said Johnny was too big. Making babies with him wasn't an option any more. Thankfully, the doctor prescribed birth control pills. As soon as he shut up, you asked to see your new son. No one believes you, but you heard him crying when they circumcised him."

CHAPTER THREE
SARA POWELL

SARA MOVED BETTY'S hand from her knee. "Do you actually think there are psychological answers on the other side you can't discover for yourself in the here and now?" Sara rarely understood the artistic nature of Nancy or Betty's troubled, empty soul. Perhaps this young doctor could at least ask them the right questions. His blue eyes were charming. And, he was focused on his task of making them all happier. The Lord knew they needed help.

Nancy Peach's son Carl had not gotten in touch for seven years. Tom, his younger brother, dismissed the guilt trips Nancy wallowed in. Tom explained at the exact time of Carl's disconnect with Nancy, Carl had experienced a life-changing trauma. Carl and his wife Pat had visited her parents in Lansing for Christmas seven years earlier. A favorite nephew of the couple overdosed on drugs. Carl must have thought his Navy training prepared him to handle the emergency. He tried unsuccessfully to revive the young man, who had died two hours earlier. Somehow Carl connected his failure to Nancy. Or, he was too defeated to admit what had happened. Carl did not initiate contact from that point on. His wife, Pat, couldn't conceive and perhaps Nancy's motherhood was too much to swallow.

As equally disturbing, Betty Pozner had lost contact with Nancy's grandson, Nik. Even though Tom, his father, was diagnosed with two incurable cancers, the fifteen-year old boy left home with his fractious mother. Betty and Nik had a long history of texting each other nearly every day. Betty reacted to the youngster's defensive cruelty as if she needed to face both the death of Tom in five years and the more immediate relationship death with Nik. His abandonment seemed the last straw in her delicate balancing act of staving off her life-threatening depression.

Sara tried to phone Nancy's grandson without any response either. So, she'd called the Seattle campus police at the University of Washington. They directed her to Nik's early college entrance program. After calling Nik in for an interview they wouldn't comment on, the Robinson Center told her to contact the Seattle police for a Welfare Check. The officer who showed up made a cursory effort, leaving a note on Nik's door to call his grandmother. Of course, Nik never contacted Nancy, Betty or Sara. Somehow the effort Sara made did lessen a degree of worry for Betty. At least someone was doing something to alert authorities that an underage, fifteen-year-old living off campus by himself was isolating from his entire family, even his mom, and classmates.

Poor Nancy rode an undulating surf of polite praise about her paintings until she went under on the next wave of self-hatred. Nothing adequately pleased her need for recognition. Trying to convince Nancy that humility was more appropriate than outlandish aspirations, failed to stifle her escalating mood changes.

Belief in the Lord's love and power had relieved most

of Sara's rejection fears and harsh realities throughout the years, but she hadn't reached Nancy or Betty with her experience of serenity. Betty was prescribed an antidepressant to stop her frightening suicidal thoughts. Nancy didn't have the sense of a brainless rabbit to curb her unacceptable demands for constant praise. Perhaps this new avenue of hope, a séance would reach them. Did any religion condone such inquiries into the afterlife?

Nancy's Catholic upbringing and Betty's rejection of Bible Fundamentalism left Sara without any belief for decades. Sara acknowledged being an alcoholic was motivation enough to return to her Savior and His daily comfort. Maybe that's why the Lord said the weak would inherit the earth. They needed to call upon Him, daily. And what if religion was a crutch, at least Sara could walk upright as a believer.

* * *

1940, Huntley White Face Ranch, Illinois

It could have been the white porcelain kitchen table Sara remembered, complete with a red strip of painted trim and a utility drawer on the long side. Maybe the nearness of boiling water or the pump at the sink; whatever the reason, the event did not take place in a comfortable double bed or at a decent hospital. Here in the kitchen, the messiness of birthing fluids would be easier to clean up after her mother's first home birth.

The first two girls, Etta and Jean, were born at a sterile, efficient hospital—painless. But Mother's sister-in-law was a nurse, and the doctor was on his way. Perhaps the pain made her more pliable than usual, hoping they would take pity on her. But there Mother was, heels on two high-backed dining room chairs, which were securely roped to the sturdy metal table, pillows under her head—and the pain. Mother heard the doctor push open the swinging door from the dining room just as she gave her last push and scream.

"Is it a boy?" the doctor asked the aunt.

Daddy, in the next room, heard the garbled words above the screams as "It's a boy!" He was relieved. The screaming finally stopped and he was happy to own his first son—his namesake.

But the child's bottom chilling on the wet metal table belonged to a girl. Sara screamed, terrified at her unwelcome reception.

It took four years to convince Mother to get near another prospect of birth, in other words to have sex with her husband.

Sara grew amidst the turmoil. The fights for sexual rights were turned into fights about why a mother could hate her own child, neglect it, ignore it.

Mother didn't know the answer. Although she could see her husband's obvious sexual tension and know its cause; she also knew even when she tried, Sara was someone she could have willingly eliminated from her life. Sara cried more than her first two and Mother knew she was at fault.

At age two Sara nearly drowned within Mother's reach. Mother had been dutifully watching the older girls swim with Sara napping behind her in the sand. But Sara had toddled into the water behind Mother. When Daddy arrived, Sara was floating face down not breathing. Everyone consoled Mother and said accidents happened, but Daddy brought it up in fights—when he was wrong and wanted to balance things out.

Then chicken pox and scarlet fever her older sisters

brought home their first month in another new school further conspired against Sara. The doctor visited saying the girls would be fine and, of course, the little one would get it too—not to worry. But Sara started to shake from convulsions by the time the doctor came back. Mother tried to restrain Sara as if she were naughty, tying her feet and arms to the bed. She heard the doctor tell Daddy she was exhausted. Sara did survive. Mother now thought Sara was even uglier, cross-eyed and dragging one foot—somewhat deaf. Her eardrum was punctured and constantly drained.

    Daddy dragged Sara from doctor to doctor, trying to fix the eye with a patch which wouldn't stay put and for endless doctoring of her ear. The foot seemed to heal. She walked a little differently, but unless you knew you couldn't tell anything was wrong. The doctor said brain damage was a possibility from the high fever. He suggested Sara should memorize things to improve her brain. Sara learned to recite all the catholic prayers, Ten Commandments, and the Credo by the age of four. Dyslexic, Sara connected the prayers to the printed words in her Sunday missal, thereby learning to read on her own.

    Mother did pity the child, entertaining her with library books. Sara was quieter, playing with her hair over the damaged left ear and looking through the books.

    Mother noticed other things were always happening since Sara's birth. Bad things. Like Daddy being chased by other women: the hired-hand's girl, the neighbor's wife. She knew she wasn't performing her conjugal duty and suspicioned Daddy's honor. She told Grandma Kerner, the tough little Hungarian, about the hired girl. The next thing Mother knew, her five brothers and four brothers-in-law were beating up Daddy in the front yard. In fact, Grandma was clubbing Daddy with the business end of a broom.

Mother intervened and they went home.

Mother nursed Daddy's bruises. He swore he had never wanted anyone but her, had never touched anyone, and would die before he would, even if they never had sex. Mother made love to him then and they had the long awaited baby boy.

Sara became even more of a demanding pain. Etta was blonde, blue-eyed and born on the Fourth of July. She looked like a princess holding out the hem of her skirt as if to curtsy. And she loved her fat cuddly baby brother. Jean, born on Memorial Day, was a worker, playing mother to anything moving, a billing and cooing child, all smiles and nicety, with thick black hair and round, brown button eyes. But Sara was embarrassingly ugly, apt to stare unashamed through her thick glasses with the one eye still disconcertingly crossing as she tried to focus. And most often you had to repeat everything to her, ruining even a pleasant acknowledgement.

Sara had a mean streak in her too. Although she seemed to love her younger brother, Sara was always breaking something important or making noise—or just about. Daddy tried to help, calling Sara in to watch her brother nurse, but Mother said she was scaring the baby, so Daddy led her away.

About this time Sara began to speak non-stop, in long sentences to get attention. There wasn't a moment's peace in the house, and she taught her little brother Lee naughty tricks, too. Lee had a speech impediment so only Sara could understand him. Lee's tongue didn't reach the roof of his mouth. Daddy pointed out that Sara made up most of what she said Lee wanted. But Lee depended on Sara, almost coming between Mother and her favorite.

Now even when Mother sang to Lee in his play table

feeding him mashed food, he would scream for his "Me," Sara, to come play with him, "Dee." It was disappointing and Mother became even more resentful, colder, and more distant.

Laying on the daybed, a wide expanse of brown and yellow linoleum separated Sara from her mother's singing to Lee in the kitchen. With the smell of tomatoes being canned and with her sisters still at school, experience had taught Sara she would lunch alone, and be alone to scratch her ear and sleep.

The round sun-warmed dining table was still a sea of lined yellow paper and blunted pencils. Earlier, the farm owner's wife encouraged Sara to print her name. But Sara didn't like to see her name spelled out, her sisters had exotic Hungarian names—Etta Madelyn, and Jean Loretta—while her own sounded and looked plain.

About the same time, right before Sara started kindergarten, a married couple—really just the husband, took notice of her in church. It was Sara's first communion. She was the youngest, so the priest had her stand up in the middle of his sermon to recite all her prayers, the Ten Commandments and the Credo. Mother had blushed. The neighbors thought out of pride, but it was shame at having such an ugly thing for a daughter. Sara's crossed eyes were magnified behind thick huge glasses. At least the other two daughters were charmers.

Anyway, this man from the town of Huntley, Illinois, visited the farm about once a week to buy fresh produce or eggs. Sara would sit on the high fence which saved the trees from the show horses. Her Daddy could make a horse sit down and even count. The man would listen to her. She would transform herself at the ear of even this casual listener into the perfect coy woman child, complimenting him on his strength, his height, his voice, his intelligence—anything to keep him there to feel a power over him.

Sara was five and he was honorable. He'd lost his baby son and all his dreams. Here was this obvious wonder, probably a genius, all those words and winsome. He was sure his wife's heart would be moved by the little saint whose family obviously did not care for her. So he asked permission to have Sara stay overnight to bring her to church the next day. Mother seemed overly relieved. Sara grew quiet, curious and shy. His wife didn't take to her. "Cross-eyed," she deemed Sara. It was true, but they were straightening out some with the new glasses.

It had been a bad idea, nothing could replace their son. So he gave Sara a cloth pin of a little Mexican boy and girl. Sara liked it. But his wife took it back, saying they didn't have presents to give her brother or sisters.

Shortly thereafter, Sara heard about an unmarried girl having a baby. She wondered what need there was for a God if he couldn't arrange for children to be born into families. Of course Sara had dreamt of being adopted away from her cold family.

Somehow she got hold of an electrical wire which wasn't grounded at the windmill water pump. They had to pull her off, and she survived a slight coma. They moved shortly after. On the new farm there was a neighbor boy her age. He followed her like a puppy and he listened. And so it went, Sara learned to get attention by courting disasters.

Daddy was dyslexic, could barely read, but knew he was intelligent. As a farm manager, he was often given commands in a demeaning tone, which would drive him crazy. When she was six, the day before another move, Sara found a place between bedroom floorboards to hide the razor strop Daddy hit them with. The offense had happened in the empty parlor. After Christmas she held a doll by its head in her outstretched arm swinging it around until the head came off. She was angry at the difference in presents. Lee received the better present, a bright red metal fire engine with a movable ladder and steering wheel. Sara had a fresh memory of running away from Daddy, around the banister of the stairwell and how easily he leapt over it to catch her and use the belt. So with this temper-ridden father and an unloving mother, Sara was raised in seven houses in eight years

Sara was well churched. Her mother's uncle was a priest and her aunt died of tuberculosis in a convent. So Etta was cloistered for two years. When she was ten, Sara put pebbles in her shoes and walked up and down the staircase to redeem the souls of those languishing in purgatory. One trip made her decide those souls would need to look elsewhere for help. Lee entered the seminary at fourteen. He left before his final vows when he was twenty-one.

CHAPTER FOUR
BETTY POZNER

BETTY CLOSED HER EYES for a second. She wanted to blank out the psychologist long enough to get a grip before he intruded into their lives more than he already had. Either his blue eyes or the tone of his deep voice seduced them into listening intently. Betty's very first cognitive therapist had straightened out a lot of their wrong ideas. He concluded their bisexual husband explained their lack of feeling loved. The resulting exploratory behavior with the opposite sex to prove their attractiveness could be the seat of their anxiety.

"We want answers before we make any more mistakes. While seeking pleasure, we often end up playing power games. Nancy likes the children more than the act of producing them. Sara receives enough material from our adventures for torrid romance books but she writes cozies. We married four times, but Sara found commitment with Powell, which doesn't mean she's happy every day. Sometimes she's sad and he's not. Nevertheless I trust Sara and Powell to behave tomorrow as they do each day. Or the Wellbutrin is working really well. Downright depressing to only have hindsight?"

"You're a lovely person," Betty said to Rick, watching Sara choose a cluster of seedless grapes from the tea chart. "Maybe a little too giving of yourself."

Betty hoped Rick appreciated Nancy's artistic pursuits and would encourage Sara to continue seeking answers, even if it was to flesh out her fictional characters. She ate a few of Sara's grapes, holding them in her right hand. "You do know we've tried all kinds of therapists?" She sipped her tea, took another a grape and sipped more tea before saying, "The first one after our stomach was pumped, heard we gathered material for Sara's books. That therapist asked, 'Why, don't you have any imagination?'"

"Paul LeDuc, a leader for another suicide-prevention group session pulled out every self-analysis trick he could find. We meditated together weekly trying to find stress points in our bodies. And, we shared stories of family woes and inner turmoil. After one doleful recitation we attempted to hug the speaker, who rebuffed us angrily. LeDuc said he should have warned us. The woman hated to be touched. Sad. We need conjoining to reinforce boundaries rather than letting our souls extend to the ends of the universe. Why did most of the women relate sexual abuse scenarios from family members?"

For years Betty thought they were free of any such occurrence. However, reminiscing with her favorite male cousin, she happened upon a repressed memory.

Butch had said, "Father Pascal and Grandpa both had a sense of humor."

Betty remembered only dour looks from both of them. The next morning, the unpleasant memory of Grandpa's indiscretion had presented itself.

Betty placed her cup on the end table and dusted off her hands. "Later we remembered when we were nine—

when Mother fell from a hayloft and broke her pelvis. She must have tried to commit suicide."

Sara chose a chocolate dipped strawberry from the tray. "Tell him about moving every year in grammar school."

Rick pulled up a pillow and sat on the other side of coffee table. His head was lower than Betty's as if he hoped to inspire confidence from his seated position instead of towering over them while he was standing.

Keeping eye contact with Rick, Betty swiped at Sara's strawberry and then licked off the smudge of chocolate from her fingers. "Daddy didn't know about dyslexia. Very intelligent, he worked as a farm manager before becoming a house painter. We moved every year. What else would cause him to fly off the handle and get fired when anyone talked down to him?"

Sara said, "I didn't know I was dyslexic until an editor pointed out the clues in my writing. She was surprised I was so well read. When we were guests anywhere, Mother would say, 'Just give her a book and she'll be quiet.'"

"Sara, you interrupted Betty telling us about her father's abuse." Rick tipped his head toward Betty.

"No, no. Daddy would have cut off both arms rather than touch us inappropriately. We always cry now when we see a father hugging a daughter. No, not Daddy. See, after Mother's accident." Betty stroked her inner thigh. "Or the suicide attempt of our friendless mother. She broke her pelvic bone, which required farming us out to various relatives." Betty coughed. "We finally ended up with our maternal grandmother, who showered us with affection. Busy on the farm, Mother rarely had time to even notice us."

Rick rubbed his forehead. "All three of you might be as dyslectic as your father."

Betty handed Sara the plate of strawberries, putting off her story for a heartbeat. "With Grandma at church, Grandpa came into our bedroom, had us sit behind him and forced us to fondle his sexual apparatus. He probably threatened to call us liars if we told anyone. Aren't most children terrified?"

Finishing a bite of strawberry, Sara said, "At least Betty wasn't raped."

"Nevertheless." Rick shook his head. "Repressed memories stay buried until we're ready, willing and able to deal with them. Going through something so horribly traumatic does leave psychological scars. Children usually fail to convince eight different adults before they are believed."

Nancy said, "Betty's marriages can just be linked to Grandpa's taking advantage of her."

Rick rumpled his brown curls. "He certainly didn't leave a good impression of the male gender."

Betty shrugged. "As we told you, Daddy didn't hug us. But after the family got back together, he worked as a janitor for a church in Crystal Lake and mother cleaned house for the nuns. We must have avoided or been unusually shy around Daddy, because for Christmas he made a wooden doll house just for us. Later, when we had stayed on the Rossmoor farm for three years, Jean said we should set the doll house curtains on fire. We were outside, thankfully. But it put an end to Daddy's special present for us. Jealous, right?"

Sara was the first to break the silence. "Betty, tell him about LeDuc."

Betty undid the red clip Sara had fixed to her hair. "Okay. Let's tell first about one of the women in the therapy group. We thought her a confidant, but the friendship offer failed the reciprocation test. She told us we talked and changed subjects too fast for her to keep up. One of her only friends, Mary Jo, ended up hospitalized after trying to gas herself in LeDuc's kitchen oven. A local priest had seduced her. We visited the priest house for an explanation. Of course, the host greeted us without his pants."

Sara played with the diamond studded cross hanging on a gold chain around her neck. "That's another reason I was an atheist for ten years. Once when Betty met LeDuc on the street, he told her he loved her and then told her he was God."

"Let us tell it," Betty said. "You ruined the punch line. We met LeDuc in the street one time in Elgin. He wanted to know why we'd quit the group. When we didn't answer, he said, 'I'm God. I love you.' We beat on his chest with our fists, telling him, 'You're married.' LeDuc repeated the same incantation over and over, 'I'm God. I love you. I love you. I am God.'"

"Finally we listened and answered him, 'You're saying God is love?'"

When Betty took a deep breath, Sara said, "She never returned to the group, realizing that was all LeDuc had to teach."

Betty felt their throat constrict. They didn't want to cry in front of Rick, but hoped he realized how fragile their self-image as women was. Why were they feeling all this pain as if for the first time? She coughed to clear their dumb throats before saying more out loud.

"Tell him about Nik," Sara said.

"Can't right now," Betty said. "Can we wait until later when we calm down?" She patted her thigh until she regained her equilibrium. "We would like to live together. They count on me. At the end of the day we like to review what's happened. Sometimes we use Sara's dreamscape to record our actions. She's quite shocked at times. Sex can be selfish. We couldn't be bothered with keeping track of our dates in our heydays. If it was Friday or Saturday night, we would dress up for dancing and exit with the first person who drove up."

"One Monday morning a guy called us at work for a lunch date. He reminded us we missed his arrival for a date—not our first chastisement for irresponsibility. Our mates agreed about our brusque and critical nature—merely efficiencies for the time allowed to sexually function. This guy said he'd decided to marry another woman because we didn't show up. We congratulated him but felt sorry for his new bride. How would you like being second best for the rest of your life?"

Sara said, "I did incorporate your plot lines and the stories people tell you about themselves into my fiction. However their faces and names all blur together because of my dyslexia."

Betty stared into space. "We try to keep a calendar now for Sara and Nancy but they often forget what's written down or don't look at the schedule at all. They should every morning, don't you think? Making decisions quickly is a sign of low intelligence, but no decision is worse than a wrong one. Speaking of intelligence and switching subjects quickly, can you keep up? We once stopped seeing a man because of the boring life promised by him. We're quick to judge confused people as being stupid. Sometimes folks are overwhelmed with too much input, as if their brains get overloaded. However we did need a brilliant mind to understand us. Sara married Powell because he is a world class mathematical physicist, but when he doesn't want to discuss something, he tells us so. That's the end of it. Sara's forced to speak to Nancy's children or her AA sponsor. At least we always had a therapist on-stage or in the wings for us. We hope this Welbutrin or your séance antics will relieve the need for such humiliating choices in the future. Are you up to the challenge?"

CHAPTER FIVE
RICK FITZGERALD

THE SYMBIOTIC RELATIONSHIPS of the three personalities presented Rick with a mind-field of possibilities. The baffling answers he might pull out of the cosmos or the other side of their shifting realities nearly discouraged his efforts.

To reset the stage, Rick pushed the tea cart to the open door. At the opposite side of the room, he opened the louvered shutters to the side bar. Mirrors behind the various liquor bottles caught beams of the lowering sun shimmering on the icy snow-covered lake. "Time is flying. Could I offer you something stronger than tea?"

Nancy was the first to perch on one of the red cushioned bar stools. "You think a brandy stinger would just hit the spot."

Sara intervened. "Kahlua and cream might be easier on your stomach."

Betty moved to the other end of the bar. "Do you know how many shots of one-hundred proof liquor you're intending to down?"

Rick ignored the interference of Betty and Sara and

fixed Nancy the drink she requested. Nancy would be the easiest to subsume. Her acceptance of her role as a mother to her boys wasn't concrete enough to uphold much added responsibility. Encouraging her to pursue her unrewarding career as an oil painter, might further aggravate her estrangement from her friends.

Nancy smiled at him when he handed her the potent mixture. She licked her left index finger after setting the overflowing glass on the bar.

She could easily be encroached upon by Betty's unhealthy but tempting sexual fantasies. Could Rick dash Nancy's hopes of personhood by having her mother say Nancy was only adequately prepared to pursue painting as a hobby to pass the time?

Betty was the real problem. Her rude behavior to Sara could not easily be set aside as casual intimacies. And her experience with various unsuccessful attempts to therapeutically relieve her anxieties about partnering with men, would limit the full utilization of her more wholesome personality traits. Her hidden resentments made her a violent person waiting for a vulnerable spot to attack any male's confidence. Her habit of ending any discourse with a question telegraphed her low self-esteem, resulting from her grandfather's initial abuse. Betty's use of the plural pronoun complicated direct confrontation.

Rick moved down the bar to serve Betty. "What would you like to drink?"

"Should we take Sara's suggestion of Kahlua and cream?"

Could Betty's search for answers be developed to bring her closer to the truth of her friendships with Nancy and Sara? Perhaps calling upon the oneness of all their souls would sound too religious for her to accept.

Sara nodded at him. "None for me. I've been sober for nearly thirteen years. Are you joining them for a drink?"

Rick nearly choked. *Joining* them was entirely what he envisioned as the answer to all their problems. "No, I need to keep my brain on high alert."

Healthy it was that Sara had been sober for so long. Her accepting nature was also a hopeful sign. Both of her friends appreciated her encouragements. Did she possess the needed mettle to guide Betty and even Nancy through the séance sessions?

He hoped their attendance would enable them to learn more about their real potential.

Nancy's constant use of the word 'just' underscored her tentative place in the scheme of things. The threesome had a leader, a follower, and a drag on their highest ideals. Sara was the leader, Nancy the follower, and Betty the constant negative element.

CHAPTER SIX
BETTY POZNER

BETTY WAVED HER HAND to include her bar mates. "They both know my therapist litanies."

She studied her drink, remembering when they worked for an architectural-engineering firm in Jackson. A fellow secretary had confided she'd been a redhead, but decided to dye her hair black at the promptings of her husband. While they were typing away at their desks, an overhead fluorescent light fell on top of the other secretary's head. Slightly injured, the young woman resumed her work that day, but months later she turned to ask Betty, "Do you see the devil coming out of my hand?"

"Get your purse," Betty directed before accompanying her to a local therapist who Betty had been using as a rent-a-friend. After the incident Betty felt saner and told the therapist she was fixed.

"What did I do or say that worked?" the clueless therapist asked.

Unsure, Betty told him, "I think you were here simply to listen to us."

Months later, Betty met the young therapist by accident. He was waiting for them outside the public restroom building of a highway rest-stop. "I wanted to tell you about your friend," he'd said. "She will be permanently hospitalized for a chemical brain malformation."

Why had he found it necessary to tell them the confidential diagnosis and why was he hanging around a highway rest-stop to speak to them? Nevertheless, they had to agree with him. Maybe the black hair dye combining with the fluorescent chemicals produced an adverse mental reaction, which could not be solved with therapy.

Betty swallowed the rest of her drink. She handed the glass to Rick. "Refill, please?"

The negative silence surrounding them allowed Betty to replay one more scenario of unsuccessful therapy.

A pair of flakey therapists in Jackson failed miserably when Betty was married to their second husband, Ken. However, the female partner did convince them to go back on the birth-control pill. The male therapist insinuated they were unhappy because they were not having enough sex. They told him he was thinking with his male organ; although they'd used the more descriptive word.

Betty straightened on the bar stool, remembering a dictate of DuKane's marketing manager, "Knockers up," which meant to thrust their remaining cleavage up for further notice.

"Why do we have this addiction to therapists, doc? The most recent diagnosed us with SAD—seasonal affect disorder. We take more vitamin D than most people and we bought a Happy Light from Ace Hardware. When our grandson stopped contacting us, we went back to her, but she palmed us off on a psychiatrist for medication.

"The therapist scared us, enlightening us about the chances of survival. The first suicide attempt gives the patient a twenty-five percent chance of accomplishing suicide. Johnny's coldness to Nancy triggered the first. The second effort guarantees a fifty percent hazard. Danny Bianco's breaking into our apartment initiated needing our stomach pumped.

"The last visit caused by Nik's moving out with his hate-filled mother, promised a seventy-five percent rate of our annihilation. We wanted to persist through another rough winter, so we agreed with the psychiatrist, who said he didn't know how we'd lasted this long without medication. We're on Welbutrin now. Are you able to stop at least our therapy addiction?"

"That's what we all hope," Rick said. "The first step in curing any addiction is to admit you are powerless over the compulsion."

"Sara and Nancy want to be relieved from listening to us spill our guts every few months." Betty's constant smile stiffened.

"The next step," Rick said, "is to believe a Power greater than yourself might help you."

Sitting between Nancy and Betty, Sara nearly gagged on her soda as she spit out, "She's not a believer!"

Betty smiled. "Rick, could we use *you* as the temporary source of a cure?"

Rick patted her shoulder. "There is a Power greater than any knowledge I possess."

"We'll borrow yours then."

"I think you just admitted you are willing to turn your life and your will over to the care of a Higher Power." Rick closed the shutters of the bar.

Betty swung her seat on the stool to face the windowed side of the room. The sun, dipping toward the rim of the iced-over lake, reflected off the sparkling sculptured ripples toward the shore.

Rick said. "We'll need to explore any character flaws which caused your trips to therapists."

"Sounds painful," Betty said, as she dismounted the bar stool. "But we might help Nancy and Sara to stop losing friends. Why have we lost touch with all or most of our lovers?"

Nancy sniffed. "You hesitate saying you might have even held onto the secretary acquaintance with the mean husband, whose son just shot himself in his mouth in a botched suicide attempt. When you helped the breakfast program for the homeless at St. Andrew's, he attended regularly. Since his speech was muddled, you were the one he would talk too. Besides his mother and you worked at the University. You failed the attempt to remove his mutilated expression out of your head. You'd be vacuuming at home and he would present himself in your mind. Anyway you stopped serving the homeless in self-defense. You heard his mother retired and then died in Florida. She was probably eight years younger than you."

Betty laughed. "We can't make miracles quite yet. She's dead, right?"

Sara asked. "I told Etta and Jean moving to Florida was a bad idea, would you set a fresh peach out in the sun or keep it in the refrigerator? I hope I live longer by staying in Michigan. Betty, how are you going to reinstate my critique partners?"

"Well one moved to a California assisted-living facility to be near her son," Betty frowned. "You don't want the responsibility of having her return, do you?"

"No. The return of my last Christmas card to another

friend who did the same thing must mean she's deceased, too. I guess they don't get mail in Heaven. Thank the Lord, Judy is still alive and happy where she's living now. Maybe I'll see her when I visit Nancy's son in the spring. What about the two Christian writers and all the other romance writers?"

"We admit our language and our way of thinking may have put them off," Betty said. "But find some of the other writers out there who want their work read."

Sara hugged herself. "When you get your dander up about some trivial incident, people react to your tirades with anger toward me. When I was the judge for a Michigan romance contest, another member named Jody tried to insert her friend at the last minute as the winner. You mailed out news to the winner you had chosen, completely disregarding Jody's choice. It's not the way I would have responded to the situation. Some of the group's members told me they thought I was a nice person and were surprised by your aggressive actions. I left the group for a year, hoping they would forget about it. Luckily, you haven't met the writing partners I have left, but they don't critique. At the City Club we just listen to each other's work."

Betty almost sobbed, but controlled herself. "Blake's poem 'A Poison Tree' should be recited more often. Do you know it, Rick?"

Rick smiled. "I don't. Do you remember all the lines?"

Betty's tone lowered with the serious words,

"I was angry with my friend; I told my wrath, my wrath did end.

I was angry with my foe: I told it not, my wrath did grow.

And I watered it in years, night and morning with my tears;

And I sunned it with smiles, and with soft deceitful wiles.

And it grew both day and night, till it bore an apple bright.

And my foe beheld it shine.

And he knew that it was mine.

And into my garden stole when the night had veiled the pole;

In the morning glad I see my foe outstretched beneath the tree."

Nancy struck her chest. "You liked every truth but the stanzas after 'and he knew that it was mine.'"

CHAPTER SEVEN
SARA POWELL

SARA RESTLESSLY HAD MOVED from the bar stool, too. She walked around the charming room and chose another cluster of seedless grapes from the tea chart near the door. She hoped Rick appreciated Nancy's artistic side and would even encourage Betty to continue seeking answers to assuage her clinical depression. Were their personalities able to ride the waves of change? As a writer, Sara sought to develop her fictional characters first from their false identities, then through glimpses of true essence, vacillating between the two states to assume the full measure of possibilities, even if they reverted a final time before transforming into their true selves.

Rick broke into her thoughts. "How did the three of you meet?"

Nancy laughed. "You don't remember. When did you first know about each other? Just recently? Do you remember, Sara?"

"We've been close since childhood," Sara said. She shook out her scarf then refolded it over her neatly placed gloves, which were laid palm to palm—as if praying. "My first friend was Sally, but Nancy and Betty never met her."

Nancy shook her head.

But Betty's eyes brightened. "The brave child who pushed you around?"

"She did not." Sara defended Sally to stop Betty in her tracks. "Sally was there when I needed her. We'd take long walks in the pasture when Daddy was still a farmer."

"He sent the dog after us at dinner time," Betty said.

It was Sara's turn to laugh. "He did. The dog, we called Carl, would politely shepherd me back to the house without my realizing his maneuvers."

"Is that why you baptized your first son Carl?" Nancy asked.

"It is!" Sara touched her cheek affectionately. "Tom was named for the first boy I ever kissed. I was sixteen on a high-school trip to the East. I met Thomas Immanuel Tucker in the moonlight on a Potomac River tour boat. We wrote for a few months. He was from Georgia and owned a white stallion. I think I still have his photograph somewhere."

Nancy pouted. "You informed yourself Johnny wanted the boys to just have simple names so no one could harass them in school."

"That was true, too. I told John the name Tom came from his Uncle Thomas Burress," Sara said. "I used my brother's name, Lee, as his second name."

Nancy giggled. "Tom and you badgered Carl, teasing him about his middle name Sylvester. Made him madder than a wet hen. Isn't that a silly cliché? How few of you have seen a wet hen? Carl always assumed you loved Tom more than him, but it wasn't accurate. You were scared when Carl was born. The birthing was easy, but you had no idea how to raise a child. Once, Johnny entered the baby's room when Carl wouldn't stop crying loudly while you were washing him. John said, 'I think he's clean enough; he's turning blue from the cold.'"

"You would get Carl all excited when Johnny came home to establish, you guess, a hook in Johnny's interest—which was waning. When you were originally pregnant Johnny acted as if some parasite was growing in you daily. You were still working. One co-worker stopped you to say he thought all pregnant women were beautiful. It helped."

"You think part of Carl's bonding problem with you started when you made his day reliant on Johnny's return from work. When you moved to Ann Arbor, Johnny's traveling job prevented his returning home more than every other weekend. Carl suffered. You remember him explaining after our separation, 'I'm sad all the time.' You should have sent him immediately to a therapist. You paid attention to Tom when he told you he was pushing on his eyes to make himself blind. That was between the second and third divorce. Tom had said, 'I don't want to see how poor we are.'"

Rick shook his head. "Parenthood is hard on couples. Tanya and I have tried for ten years to have children. I think my mother thought we were acquiring wealth and avoiding the prospect of paying for a child's upbringing. I finally told her we were losing money on failed fertility treatments. We don't know what the Lord has planned for us in the future."

Sara said, "What's wrong with adopting? The world is full of children wanting a family to call their own."

Rick sighed. "We haven't given up having our own. Tanya wants the child to be hers. She's afraid we might not bond with a stranger."

Nancy continued, "Tom was born at nine pounds fifteen ounces, quite an ordeal. Anyway when you brought him home, he could hold his head up. He looked around the apartment as if evaluating his home. He was beat up in the birthing process and his black brittle hair reached his shoulders. When Mother saw him for the first time, she said, 'It's all right. We can cut his hair.'"

"Shortly after, you moved into your first home. You had a double bed in Tom's nursery. You weren't afraid he would break. You would lie on the bed to throw him up in the air and catch him. You think Johnny was jealous of your bond. Maybe Carl was too. But the real ordeal happened after a second reconciliation attempt when Johnny asked the boys which parent they wanted to live with. Tom said he'd lived with Johnny during the divorce. Now he wanted to live with you. Johnny and you had agreed the boys wouldn't be separated. Carl was never happy with the arrangement. Maybe when you got Carl all excited about Daddy arriving home every day, he really missed him when we moved to Ann Arbor, where Johnny had the four-state selling job. Tom understood you before you spoke, but Carl was always mystery to you. Still is. Carl professes to be a believer, but apparently he hasn't read, 'Honor thy father and thy mother.'"

"Johnny passed three years ago. Tom was with his dad, but by the time Carl believed his father was seriously ill, it was too late. Johnny was unconscious when Carl arrived to say good-bye. You know it shows your resentment, but you hope he doesn't show up at your end to ask forgiveness for shunning you. But you'll probably just forgive him if he does arrive in time."

Rick looked at the floor as if he didn't know how to respond.

Sara changed the subject, "I stopped using, I mean

befriending, Sally when I started high school. I switched to loving a white rental horse named Flicka."

"Was the horse your rent-a-friend therapist?" Betty made herself comfortable on the couch.

Sara shook her head. "I rode with an English saddle every weekend it didn't rain. The stable boys told the owner I had a natural seat, but they warned me to not ride so fast. My heart flew when Flicka and I were galloping along the trails. The best part of the ride was Flicka's rocking canter gait." Sara patted the couch next to her, inviting Rick to join them.

Rick chose the low pillow on the other side of the coffee table, again.

Sara leaned forward to continue her story. "One time my best high-school friend, Judy Wisnewski, joined me. Judy rode English too, but she had learned a four rein method of guiding the horse. Flicka had one flaw—she never allowed another horse to pass her." Sara laughed. "I explained to Judy, adding Flicka's ears would flatten if she was getting upset. Sure enough when the trail widened somewhat in the field before a stand of trees, Judy's high-stepping horse wanted to lead the group. Flicka reacted by kicking sideways, smashing Judy's wooden stirrup. Judy never asked to ride with me again."

"That must have been disappointing," Rick said.

"She didn't understand. Flicka had rules. Aren't we supposed to respect our friends' way of doing things?"

Betty huffed. "She was only a horse."

"A friend is just a friend." Nancy hunched forward. "Animal or human."

Sara scooted back on the couch. She let her head lean back, resting her neck on the pillows. "I've always felt more loved by animals than humans."

"Nonsense," Betty said. "Animals follow you around, pretending attention, because you're the source of their food. They're all parasites."

Rick noticed Sara appeared unruffled by Betty's words. "Who is your best friend, Betty?"

"Not one," Betty answered. "I'm blessed with two."

Nancy twirled the hair near her ear, but then Sara spread her arms out along the tops of the pillows. "Betty, I realize why you don't believe in a Higher Power. You're too independent to rely on anything or anybody—other than your own efforts."

"True," Betty said. "When things get tough, we get tougher. Unfortunately. Do you think we're increasingly hard-hearted?"

Rick drummed his fingers on the coffee table. "And when it's time to love, the solidified heart isn't able to soften."

"Well at least God doesn't require love, does He?" Betty asked.

Nancy spoke up quickly. "Oh yes He does. Why else would the Lord bother making you? The black emptiness in the beginning was just too lonely, so He produced listeners for His words."

Betty fluffed her hair. "We can understand. Don't we all need an audience to please?"

"In the Beginning was the Word." Silently, Sara celebrated the steps her friends were making toward accepting the Lord. Perhaps she'd misjudged Nancy. Maybe the artist in Nancy did recognize the first Creator of all. Betty's strides to rid herself of therapy sounded pretty close to recognition of someone or something outside of herself, too. *Judge not that ye be not judged*, played its familiar tune in her head. For Sara, writing was somewhat like the Lord's reason for creation. She extended her tentacles of awareness into each soul she met or created in order to grow, the way the Lord changed when Lot argued with him, or when He reacted in anger to Job sharing his suffering. Besides without writing, Sara felt she had no meaning or purpose in life.

Rick ran his fingers through his curls, again. "Did you answer me about first meeting, yet?"

"No," the three of them chorused.

"I knew Sally," Betty said.

"I was young," Sara said, "when she was my imaginary friend."

Nancy spoke quietly. "You just met you all at the City Club for a Morning Musicale. At the table, Betty, you were talking about your grandson, Nik."

"He stopped texting us." Betty hiccupped. "Too much alcohol."

"Maybe too much emotion," Rick said.

"Why do you want to know the length of my friendships?" Sara asked.

CHAPTER EIGHT
RICK FITZGERALD

"CURIOSITY," RICK SAID. "You are all so different from each other." He got to his feet.

The night sky was dark blue. Silhouettes of black trees punctuated the lake scene. Rick pulled the drapes shut, then checked his watch. "We could begin," Rick said as he turned toward them.

Nancy started to cry. "You probably won't stay."

Betty and Sara rose from the couch with her.

"Nothing to fear," Rick said. "Please sit back down. If you're uncomfortable during the process raise your hand or speak out. Nancy, wave your left hand, Betty put your right hand up and Sara why don't you cross your arms and I'll stop speaking. Think of this as a trip to a high mountain to consult a wise sage." Rick blocked their path to the door. "We all have things to learn, right?"

"We know we do, don't we?" was Betty's habitual mode of response.

Sara took Nancy's left hand, pressing it to her lips. "I won't let anything untoward happen to you. I promise."

Nancy turned to Rick. "Just how old are you?"

"Does my age have something to do with my expertise or your confidence in my help?"

"Both," Sara said. "Nancy and Betty are so unique, I'm afraid you haven't come across similar personalities in your work."

Rick pulled on one curl near the center of his forehead. "I know you all are capable of continuing to learn about yourselves or you wouldn't be here. And my solution will guarantee all three of you will be less lonely."

Sara took a deep breath. "We can face the challenge of the unknown, can't we?"

Rick assured himself he could readily follow the shifting conversational styles. Nancy's childish tone reached its highest pitch on the word 'just'. Betty's strident questions held lower manly tones. Sara's fit her character. The well pronounced words proved Sara's extensive reading as well as her post-graduate degree. She had conquered her dyslexia.

Nancy wiped away her tears with her sleeve. "Why do you just get the sinister signal?"

"Because you're the worst?" Betty laughed.

"Left-handed people are no longer stigmatized," Sara said.

Rick was relieved when they resumed their seats on the couch. "All you were looking for might be just a moment away. Pay attention and see if you discover an answer, a reassurance, a completion."

How was he going to reach these three? He started lighting the candles around the room, slowly shutting off the lights in the process. No ventriloquist skills were up his sleeve, no hidden wires or buttons to push for special effects. He needed the women to experience enough freedom to find their own resolution in this space of promised pleasure.

He shuddered at the thought of picking up their emotional pieces if he succeeded in breaking down their eggshell defenses. Nancy, the most vulnerable of the three, would be the easiest to shatter. Betty's iron-clad defenses would be the most difficult to penetrate. Sara's listening skills, honed by her writing career, would brook no tricks from chicanery crafts.

Betty's protection devices would need to be broached first. Then Nancy's fears might diminish as she built up some trust in his methods. Of course, he felt censored by Sara's all seeing presence. This was not going to be an easy session.

The grandfather clock struck the hour, five o'clock, with the sun falling off the earth.

"Would you rather eat dinner before we begin?" Rick asked.

All three nodded their Gordian heads.

Rick excused himself to ask Tanya to bring in the room-service cart. She had planned a light dinner to keep their thinking processes unblocked. An assortment of cold cuts, slices of chicken, ham and various cheeses were laid out along with sliced portions of vegetables and fruit. All three of the guests knew Tanya, who worked as the cook at their City Club in Ann Arbor.

They clapped when Tanya wheeled in a second dinner cart filled with a selection of cakes and fruit tarts. Hot coffee was served with a diet caffeine drink available for something cooler. Always discrete, Tanya didn't join their conversation. She shut the door quietly behind her.

Nancy quickly moved across the room to open it. "You just want to be able to escape."

Rick nodded. "Could I tell you how you are similar to each other?"

"We're unique," Betty said. She'd ignored the more substantive food and filled her plate with desserts.

"You certainly are." Sara asked permission from her and daintily chose two cream puffs from Betty's selection. "I know life is short, but this is ridiculous."

Nancy set aside Betty's plate. She chose chicken and grapes from the food selection.

"Add a bit of ham and Swiss with cucumber slices," Sara directed. "I want to live until spring, at least."

"You're really not comparable," Nancy said. "Sara writes constantly, you just paint at every opportunity and Betty's calendar is filled with therapy appointments."

"All of you have the same shade of dark brown hair," Rick noted.

"Same hairstylist." Betty bit off a piece of raspberry tart.

"Tanya told me you usually coordinate your outfits." Rick indicated the herringbone pattern of their apparel.

"It happens," Sara said, unbuttoning her jacket.

"We don't call each other every morning." Betty tugged at the hem of her skirt. "If that's what you're implying."

"It's just magic," Nancy tugged at a strand of hair. "Like agreeing to arrive here, when Tanya said you would benefit from speaking to him."

"What about your shoes," Rick asked. Surely they would recognize the paucity of differentiation sometime.

"It was difficult to find herringbone patterned shoes." Sara leaned forward to survey her shoes.

"You just like them," Nancy said.

"What are you driving at?" Betty asked. "Are you implying we have an inappropriate relationship?"

"Not in the least," Rick said. "Your friendships have served you well."

"But?" Sara asked.

Rick reiterated to himself that Sara was the one who would catch on first. He hoped she wouldn't bolt with the new possibilities of the friendship. "I think you could incorporate the skills of each of you into the personalities of all of you."

"Oil paints are too messy." Betty wiped her sticky fingers on a napkin she'd dipped into her water glass. "Could we ask for something stronger than coffee?"

"Level heads," Sara cautioned. "We need to keep our wits about us."

"How do you propose to enlighten us?" Betty challenged.

Rick placed his empty plate on the bottom shelf of the cart before answering. "The Lord created you with all the answers to any question."

"So just let you ask him." Nancy's eyes were shining. "Is he going to provide a straight phone line to Mother? He won't hoodwink you. You would still recognize her voice anywhere."

"I hope to let you know in your heart," Rick said. "Exactly what your birth mother envisioned for her child."

"Answers vary with the circumstances," Betty said. "Tomorrow will we think about today's problems?"

"I think the pool of souls on the other side has already experienced your life, all its trials and clarifications in their entirety," Rick said.

"After all," Sara quoted. "'There is nothing new under the sun.'"

"For us there is," Betty said.

"You too," Nancy chimed in.

Rick understood Sara possessed the most humility of the three. Her attitude could easily incorporate his proposition for their relief. Betty still believed they could handle their own lives and poor Nancy was hanging on to a hope for the world's recognition.

"I don't believe in spirit writing," Sara said, "if that's one of your ploys."

"It isn't." Rick assured her. "Betty, you appear to us as a confident person who manages the outcome of your life choices."

"Yes?" She tilted her chin up.

"Nancy, your insecurity takes away from your accomplishments. Somehow your negative internal talk seeps into your outward actions.'

"How?" Nancy hunched forward.

"Sara, your empathetic nature allows everyone to relax around you."

"Glad, I am, of that." Sara smiled.

Rick realized the play was beginning. "So, Sara, tell us what you realize about these two from their actions?"

CHAPTER NINE
SARA POWELL

"RICK, I THINK YOU NEED to know more of Nancy's tendency to isolate, which is why she likes to lose herself in painting whenever Betty and I allow her a section of time. I think painting is therapy for her depression. I can't understand her need for public recognition. She might even stop painting if her acknowledgement goal was gratified. Actually, I think painting for her is a type of regression into childhood—which wasn't that happy.

"In Illinois when Nancy was ten she followed Daddy around the Rosmoor farm whenever she could. Once running to keep up with him, she pulled on his sleeve. 'Daddy,' she asked surprised to have his undivided attention. 'If I was a boy, would you love me more?'"

"Daddy pulled his arm away. A look of horror his answer. He did deign to pay more attention to Nancy coming in from the fields to ask Mother, 'But where is she? You never know where she is. Something could happen to her, again.' A great slamming about of kitchen cupboard doors would ensue.

"One time Nancy was surprised to hear her parents

describe a girl who had a child without being married. What was God for if he didn't arrange who was to raise each child? Shocking it was. There was no Divine plan for Nancy to be parented by these two cold individuals.

"Another time when Mother mopped the floor vigorously, Nancy had asked some irritating question. Mother dipped the mop into the bucket with extra force, stepping forward on the wet floor. Still holding the soapy mop in the bucket, she slipped. The bucket flipped skyward raining dirty soap suds down on her. Nancy laughed at the hilarious sight. The rift between daughter and mother was re-emphasized. From then on, Nancy never expected the slightest affirmation from Mother. It was like knowing a favorite country road had been cut in half by a freeway and didn't go anywhere anymore.

"Daddy's estrangement came later, when Nancy was about twelve. A stable manager for a famous race horse, Greyhound, who held some status among the farm owners, became Daddy's friend on the Rossmoor farm, the last farm he ever managed. Daddy loved to gab and finally won an appreciative audience. Mother would fuss and fume in the car on their weekly visits when it was clearly time to get home to milk the cows. 'Telling his whole life history again,' she would complain.

"The stable manager's house had one of the first televisions in the county, so Nancy's family would make weekend visits. Mother didn't like the man's wife, who was slimmer and ten years younger than the balding man. Once, the wife washed his remaining hair right in front of everyone. Mother always maintained a stand-offish attitude toward Daddy, who seemed content to remain the sexual pursuer.

"Classmate boys of Nancy's worked on the farm. One

evening the boys, Nancy and the old man went into town to bring back ice cream and beer. On the visor of the car were sayings which the boys kept pulling down and reading to her, laughing and carrying on like young boys do. The old man tried to stop the nonsense, but he was laughing too. He patted her knees and left his arm in her lap. One saying was, 'I'll show you my puppy if you'll show me your pussy.'

"After that trip, Nancy noticed the man usually had something to tell just her or would invite her to sit on his lap to watch television. The last time she went, it was dark in the room with an explanation that the lit screen was clearer if the room was dark. Nancy's family was there, sitting around. He was in his big deep arm chair facing toward the front with the rest behind them, except for the kids belly down on the rug. His wife seemed to be away from home.

"As Nancy climbed on his lap, he moved his hand from the arm of the chair across her stomach, pressing down somewhat. She held his big hand with her tiny fingers. Then he shifted his position, moving one hand under her buttocks keeping his hand in her crease, moving his legs when he would draw attention to something on the television. Sometimes rubbing his leg or something with his hand under her, finally her dress was no longer under her and he moved his hard part through his open pants to rest near her privates.

"Nancy resisted and tried to move away. 'Sit still,' he commanded out loud, 'I want to watch this.' Mother scolded her too, so she sat still. In the dark he moved against his clothing and hers until she felt the dampness and heard his sigh. He fell asleep, the program finished and Nancy got down in the dark as her family left to go home.

"The next time they were all in the car ready to go, she delayed and finally refused. Mother went in to drag her out, and somehow Nancy convinced her why she didn't want to go. That he had touched her. Nancy never realized the grief Daddy must have felt at the loss of a friend. Nancy was relieved not to go anymore. They bought their own television."

Rick coughed. "Nancy, how do you feel now that Sara has explained part of your bringing up?"

Sara wouldn't let Nancy into the conversation. "You haven't heard enough. Actually at that point in time Nancy felt empowered after standing up for herself. I think she borrowed Daddy's pride and Mother's piety to define the confusing world around her."

Sara tugged her skirt down before continuing. "But fate had more discouragement awaiting Nancy. Married teachers welcomed Nancy—however slightly—to visit them on her bike rides in the summer. Standing in their vegetable garden chatting away, Nancy asked the husband some questions. The sixth grade teacher replied, 'You're just like a broken record. You talk on and on.'

"That same teacher suffered at Nancy's unwitting hand. He'd lost his temper in the classroom over some boys not attending to a spelling bee and he cursed them, using the word 'damn.' Nancy told Daddy and as he retold it on the phone it was turned into, 'God damn you.' It worried her, so after the house was still, she went into their bedroom and woke him, explaining the teacher had not said, 'God damn you' only 'damn.' From then on Daddy called Nancy a liar, referring to simple statements with, 'Are you sure you didn't dream that up?' and 'We can't believe anything you say.'"

Rick asked, "Was your father linking his belief that

Nancy was a liar to the incident with the stable manager?"

Sara shook her head. "Maybe, he wanted to resume his friendship, to believe the man was maliciously maligned rather than to accept the fact that he was present while his daughter was molested. Daddy often told Nancy, 'You just like to hear yourself talk, or 'Don't tell people everything you know.' So, Nancy did stop talking until she was nineteen, when she started dating and couldn't otherwise hide her nervousness."

"High school must have been difficult for her to make friends." Rick pulled up his socks blushing as if remembering his own difficulties.

"It was," Sara said. "A young woman's parents and younger brother who occupied St. Patrick's pew in front of Nancy's family's, brought Nancy the first free thoughts about religious observances. The woman had married outside the church's approval—at that time deemed sin enough for excommunication. When she and her baby were killed in a train crash and her husband survived, the parish would not allow her to be buried in hallowed ground. The suffering of the dead girl's parents was palpable, so real you could taste it. Mother and Nancy had long arguments about the lost soul. Nancy thought the church presumptuous to assume they knew her final communication with God before she died.

"After high-school, Nancy's first job was with an electronics firm. Her sisters worked in the air-conditioned computer center. Etta and Jean played a waiting game until their wedding date or pregnancy promised early retirement. Nancy was a stenographer. On the first day, her bottom lip quivered from nervousness. The first assignment was a simple letter with five carbon copies. To correct an error in the first line, Nancy dutifully erased an entire line without damaging the paper on the original and five copies. The short man who gave her the letter said not to do that again—they had lots of paper.

"Nancy worked there three years. She dated a few men and avoided date rape while trying to convert Protestants to Roman Catholics. Then Nancy met Johnny, a six-foot-five inch giant. He said he was an Evangelical Christian from Texas, which meant he wanted to save her soul. Nancy felt she'd been saying 'no' long enough, but Johnny wouldn't go to bed with her.

"Nancy kept chasing Johnny, invited him to a girlfriend's wedding and kept courting him. Once when he was sick with the flu, Nancy brought him Mother's chicken soup. However, her parents wanted her to marry a Catholic son of a drugstore owner. She did date him, but he was the first man she explored who didn't have a hard on. Nancy thought he was broken.

"In 2008 when my husband Powell and I returned for my fiftieth class St. Charles High School reunion, this drug store was forced to close down. We learned his son had sold illegal prescriptions. The next day when we visited Nancy's old church, the druggist was sitting across the aisle for Mass. Strange how the universe wants to show the results of early decisions."

Sara rubbed her forehead in consternation. "Nancy, sometimes I want to kick you into next Wednesday, because you're so slow to recognize your talents. You bend your shoulders forward as if expecting a blow. You might as well be sucking your infantile thumb."

Rick handed Sara a tissue which she dabbed a tissue to her eyes. "When either of you talk, neither of you take time to envision how what you say affects others."

"Beautiful and sympathetic observations," Rick said.

Sara hugged herself as if she wanted to comfort her friends. "Betty wears me out. She's always on high alert, ready to object or qualify any word or deed. She struts instead of walking—and keeps her shoulders back as if her mother still had a book on her head. Mother listened to a program at breakfast which directed she march us around the breakfast table. When we began to 'bud,' I think that's the word the biology teacher used when she stared at our breasts, Mother placed a book on our heads. Back to Betty, her face assumes a rigid pose, lips narrowing, eyes glaring—although defensively, I think. To understand Betty, I need to tell you more about Nancy's marriage to John.

"In 1960 John the cross-town, Bible-toting man would not make love. Nancy thought he was honorable, but actually he wasn't interested in making love to a woman. At Nancy's instigation they did get partially intimate which slightly injured Nancy. When she explained to him, he said, 'Well, we could get married.'

"They decided to elope because of the Catholic Church's view on intermarriage. The year was 1960 when people still celebrated the Big War. The Veteran's Day parade found Nancy's parents being congratulated for marrying off their third daughter. John and Nancy didn't realize the license would be published the Thursday before their Saturday wedding. The priest and Jean showed up, demanding to know if Nancy was pregnant. After four hours of tutorials, Nancy dressed alone in the house for her wedding. The Justice of Peace was forty-five minutes late. Fifteen minutes more would have seen both John and Nancy bolting for the door. They moved to a renovated school house on Dunham Road next to the railroad tracks.

"Did Nancy love him through the early years when they rented an upstairs apartment on Arlington Avenue in

Elgin, Illinois? Absolutely. His errors were misconceptions on her part, his flirtations—someone else's sin. His indifference was her own failing, his anger her fault. Soon and not too soon for Nancy a child was being assembled—much to the horror of John. She taught her first blue-eyed blond baby boy to look forward to Daddy's arrival home from work. Soon Carl understood he was to love Daddy more than her. She had created a lopsided world.

"Nancy planned a shift in the universe in 1962. John's brother drove Nancy and Carl down to Missouri to visit Johnny's mother. Johnny and Nancy were using a foam spermicide for birth control. She made sure John knew she left the birth-control equipment at home on the pretense that she didn't want him to worry, or be jealous. John joined them after a week. He had missed her. In an old bed with a huge headboard and footboard, Nancy would never forget how he vaulted the footboard whispering, 'Here I come.' Nancy's second son, Tom, was thus conceived by her foresight.

"She became possessive of both children and overprotective. The possessiveness turned into a love of possessions. Nancy never had enough for her sons. John was relegated to provider, a nonparticipant in Nancy's emotional bank. Boredom, senseless bickering, faultfinding and misunderstandings drove out any sexual need. Loyalty and exaggerated pride disallowed Nancy from confiding her unhappiness to anyone.

"In their first home in South Elgin, Illinois, one afternoon about four years into the marriage, Nancy started packing to leave but reconsidered. John at first stormed around but while she unpacked regained his haughty indifference. He said, 'You're like a broken radio. I keep trying to fix it but soon I'll leave you on the shelf.' But Nancy laid out plans for escape, which even then didn't include her sons. Separation was probably a few months away, when John was transferred to Ann Arbor, Michigan for a traveling job.

"Husbanded one weekend a month with grammar school engulfing her oldest son, Nancy would wake up wondering what she was going to do all day. John's life during their last years together was a mystery to her. While sitting on his lap one night, she fished in his shirt pocket and found a slip of paper with the first name of a girl and a phone number. They argued about it. He took the note, drove away and came back without it. He refused to discuss it further.

"Not long after, Betty bought five new nightgowns and tried them on for his approval as a way to show him she'd forgiven him for whatever had happened. He wasn't any more interested in her than if she'd been wrapped in cement. She started to cry and he sat down on the bed next to her and began to sob. She put her arm around him, sorry for upsetting him. John shook her off, looked her right in the eye and asked, 'There. How does it feel?' Nancy was in a daze. She walked into the front room and sat down. It must be over. When John came into the room, standing on one foot then the other, she asked, 'Should we get a divorce?' 'No,' John said quite calmly. 'I just wanted you to see what I have to deal with.' The cruelty did not leave her. She blocked out the thought that he didn't love her. She accepted his verdict. She was not mature, not able to express herself. She went on with their life as best she could—for a while.

"Once, Nancy stood at the front room window staring at the huge oak that sheltered the central knoll in the school yard across the street. She prayed a final time; if there was a God could he make blue roses bloom on that oak. With all the faith she could muster Nancy prayed for blue roses as a sign that she could endure. Suicidal thoughts reminded her that survival was surely a more godly plan.

"Shortly after praying for blue roses, Nancy sat on John's lap trying to seduce him into the bedroom, promising oddly never to leave him. It was a rainy day and during intercourse, she mentioned the rain. John said, 'Who needs the weather on such a sunny day.' Nancy loved him then.

"But watching the boys with their birthday toys, Nancy remembered how they anticipated new treasures. They would assemble all their old toys and play with them, some for the first time since Christmas. They were telling their old toys goodbye. Nancy's last act of love with John seemed, even with the promise to never leave, a final kiss of goodbye to the love she once felt for him. Nancy often complained to herself that Johnny was usually tired, coming home later and later, not expecting supper. A peck on the cheek and a question about her day seemed the extent of his attention. He acted as if he were asleep before his shoes were off. John couldn't have been that exhausted all the time unless he was bored with her. She had uselessly searched for an alluring nightgown. If you wanted sex, going to bed nude should do it.

"In March of 1969 when Nancy's parents had visited them in Ann Arbor, she brought the coffee pot into the front room to replenish their cups. Once she returned to the kitchen for the cookie tray, Nancy heard Mother say to John, 'Well, I see you finally have her trained.' Nancy felt her soul turn around inside her bone structure. Betty emerged to tell her she was right to hate them all."

Rick's hands were in his curls. "Thank you, Sara. Betty did play an important role in keeping Nancy alive."

CHAPTER ELEVEN
BETTY POZNER

Winter, Big Wolf Lake, Michigan

"From what we see," Betty said, rolling her eyes from side to side. "Nancy will be the easiest to convert. She's impressionable. But don't think she's stupid."

Sara resumed her recitation of Nancy's past. "Through the next two weekends, John's job kept him on the road. When he returned he was sick with the flu for a week. He'd inherited some strange ideas about illness from a Christian Scientist on his mother's side. With a fever and diarrhea, he wouldn't bathe or drink liquids. After a week he felt better. The bedroom was rank with his body odor. He asked for sex. Betty was nauseated from his smell."

Betty interrupted. "The next morning, a Monday, he showered and packed for another stint on the road. As we handed him his suitcase at the back door, we thought, *We wouldn't care if we never had to see you again in this lifetime.*"

Sara held her hand over her face to regain control of the conversation. "Why haven't you told Rick about falling in love in 1967 with Butch?"

Betty shifted her position before answering. "We don't recall the countless Fourth of July family reunions. The events we remember rarely fall on prescribed holidays. Our emotionally-charged memories somehow bring all the light and color, sound and smells back with them. Nowhere near Valentine's Day or even properly under the freedom of divorce, we fell in love." Betty continued, "John's promotion and the move away from family and friends produced a void awaiting the incoming tide of events. Our mother's sister lived about an hour's drive from our new home in Ann Arbor. We were invited for Thanksgiving dinner. Our cousin, Butch, had just been separated and reunited with his wife. The estranged couple was not invited because of the heated words on both sides of the family. John wasn't enthusiastic about the trip. He traveled enough in his job.

"We misunderstood the instructions on how to get to the destination. Our uncle's name and cousin's name were not easily distinguishable in the gas station's phone directory. We continued searching down narrower and narrower streets until we spotted our uncle's suicide truck. That's what our father, Udale, called the big car-hauling rigs. We went to the door and out of the gloom behind him, Butch appeared. We were so thankful to recognize someone and homesick for family, we were a bit overwhelming. We gushed and explained in a few embarrassed words. Then we demanded a kissing cousin's privilege, which he freely gave. His chin was dimpled and his face as soft-skinned as our own. Aglow from a man who was at best confused, we happily got back in the car with the correct directions for our surly husband.

"About six months later, our cousin's younger brother married before he entered the service. Mother and Daddy came from Illinois. We were excited about going. At the reception Butch danced with his sister. His marriage had disintegrated again. The dance was modern and we felt outdated. Butch had a glorious figure, tight-butted, full chested with a happy spirit. He danced using his hips as we imagined he did in bed. His eyes were diamond blue and he was crowned with a curly golden tangle—he was a thing of beauty.

"For a year or two when driving was not a hazard, we and the children would visit our aunt. Butch was living there with his two baby boys. He worked in a car factory and was usually home early enough to have supper with them before we returned home. Aunt Elizabeth was a bulky woman—not the barrel type but softly cushioned. Uncle Glen possessed a lively men's-room wit. A cancerous tumor removed from his forehead left a disc-like scar. After the operation he attempted suicide, but therapy changed his mind for the family's sake. Actually, the family might have been less traumatized if he'd gone earlier. Still a victim of cancer with a year to live, we knew him as a sprightly gardening man, proud of his family, determined to shake some happiness out of life. After he'd been hospitalized for treatment in Ann Arbor, where we occasionally played cards with him, he came home without hope. With death approaching, jealous of the health of others, he was unable to tolerate children, his grandsons, without voicing his vindictiveness.

"The family was shaken. Butch could not please when it was most needed for his peace of mind and guilt-free future. Our aunt confided, 'He still wants me to go to bed with him and I can't even stand to touch him.'

"Butch had a hunting cabin up north that he wanted his dad to enjoy. But our uncle found pessimistic, negative reasons why the cabin would be useless. Hoping to influence Uncle Glen, we told Butch we would like to see it. During his summer layoff, we visited the cabin with his two toddlers and our boys. We marshaled the children through a small patch of woods. The babies were not as tall as the ferns. We retired to the cabin to wash stained hands and wipe various noses. Then with the older boys playing rangers, we forged a little further into the woods. We hadn't been this close to raw nature. Illinois held more cultivated land than forests. We came alive with all the new sensations. Butch would point out a thing of wonder—if unable to further describe it. One treed dell of his choosing had purple shadows lain on a carpet of thick moss. When fall came, John and the boys would meet Butch at his cabin for a weekend of hunting. Our inhibitions included the inability to talk to men once we'd married, but Butch was surely harmless. He was family. We drank too deeply of acceptance and it turned our head irretrievably toward the source.

"During the winter of 1969 we lived in a fiction world with a beloved to fill our thoughts. Inhaling, we smelled the wood smoke and touched the green moss, exhaling we saw Butch's sun-lit blue eyes and graceful form. As soon as spring allowed, we and the boys revisited Aunt Elizabeth. At home, John's presence became suffocating—evil and unnecessary.

"In March of 1969 we packed the kids in the back seat of the Dodge and drove north about sixty miles to visit our aunt. We won a game of chess and bragged, 'We won two games out of three the last time we played John.' But silently we recalled after winning the game, our boorish husband said he could have won earlier but had wanted us to learn more. We resignedly admitted to Butch, 'But then, no one ever beats John.'"

"Butch jumped down our throat. 'Who are you? No one? You just told me you won two out of three.'"

"Who are you, no one?" We recognized our basic question. The life was his, the marriage, house, religion, politics, friends, and children. Who were we? Non-being, non-experienced, non-living was the heart of the problem. No variance from John's ideas was permitted.

"On April 20th, 1969, we called Butch and told him we missed him—even cared for him. Butch didn't seem surprised. He accepted our declaration as his due. We met in a Flint park hidden near a lake embankment. A picnic building sheltered us from a foggy rain. We started to talk and laugh at an imagined monster in the adjoining lake. To allow more time to talk we tried to eat in a restaurant but parked in front and shredded John to ribbons. Butch explained how John repeatedly made passes at him, touching his knee under the card table, etc. We attended a drive-in movie and made love. We couldn't recognize his beauty in the dark.

"Butch had considered our position as a married woman, convenient and free of his responsibility. Our Greek god had clay feet and reality descended. We thanked our reserve for planning without considering his desires. We went home with our mind in turmoil. Wild vengeful thoughts would hold sway. Freedom was knocking at a wall of piety and pride. We proceeded to pack what we considered our belongings. We fluctuated between the fear of leaving and the call of freedom. We arranged the boy's beds together in one room, outfitting the emptied room as our sewing room. We installed the free standing hammock, planning to sleep there without causing a scandal. But the imagined emotional hell was too much for us. We continued packing, not intending to take the boys.

"We felt the ultimate consumer as if our presence was chewing up John's material goods, chairs, rugs, tennis shoes, boxes, pots, lipsticks. We saw the whirlwind we had reaped and needed to end the cycle. The last few days it was impossible to swallow or even taste solids. John had provided them and they made us nauseous. We drank only liquids—tea, soup, milk. We lost weight. No one was around to notice we reached our goal of 125 pounds.

"We knew we would miss the boys, but thought maybe three months would be the longest we wouldn't see them. We needed to provide a place for them, balked at the thought of taking any more of John's money—even to feed them. John would find a housekeeper for them right where they were, then Carl wouldn't need to change schools. John wouldn't want to raise them and we thought he'd be glad to have us take them off his hands. We made a list of housekeepers for the interim and explained our plans to a neighbor who was a state-licensed foster parent. We asked if the children could stay with them after school and through supper until John returned that evening.

"We told Carl and Tom good-bye that we were leaving their father because we were unhappy. We assured them their father loved them and would care for them until we could return. We explained we didn't want to take their father's money to feed them. We insisted they should always believe we loved them no matter what anyone else told them. Tom was five and Carl seven. It was lunchtime. Carl returned to school by way of the front door. It wasn't easy to close that door. Tom went out the patio door to play with the neighbor boy whose mother would watch him until school was over. He had to climb their fence but fell as he started over. Our heart wrenched, but we were determined to proceed.

"So long, it's been good to know you. So long, it's been good to know you. We knew we were off key and irreverent, but we were free. The 1965 Dodge Dart hugged the clover leaf of the expressway as we focused our attention on the blue sky. In a month we would be twenty-nine. We didn't look it and couldn't fathom where the time had gone. We tilted the rear view mirror but saw a guileless girl without grey in our brown waves. Our face was flushed from the excitement of fleeing. Driving away we knew there was no loving family to run to, so we headed in the direction of safe turf.

"We claimed ownership of a pasture. Our family had lived at the place for three years when we were eleven to thirteen years old. The farm house was old and each generation added a wing until the building was twice its original size. The dark woodwork, ornate staircase, nooks and crannies were romantic castle fare. The rambling two acre pasture was our humble domain. On summer mornings we would wake at first light, watching the faint outline of the utility room's roof and the chimney change colors from the eastern sun. We would climb the orange field fence as our dog, Carl, wiggled underneath. In the pasture every clump of grass, turn of the creek, angle of the tree limbs, and huge field boulders claimed us. We felt entitled to a place on the earth. Even now in flight, the sun-warmed trunk of a favorite tree called to us.

"We had lunch in Ohio under a just greening willow tree. Without supper we slept in a St. Charles, Illinois, road-side motel that night."

* * *

"When we arrived at our parents the next day, Nancy's children and John arrived from Ann Arbor. He'd driven all night. We sat in his company car and turned around to look at the boys. Carl smiled at us from the far side of the back seat. His blond hair was neatly in place. Tom grabbed our arm with all his might and pressed his dark curls against ours. The boys didn't suspect anything was wrong. Mom often did unusual things. We had missed them after one night alone. We realized the strength of the love we felt for them.

"It was physically painful to be close to John. If we could have worked some magic to make him disappear from the car, we would have used it. He was a stranger to us—as if we hadn't seen him in years. His craggy face and thickened frame were familiar, but we had no idea what he was apt to do now.

"Our father asked when they were outside where Mother couldn't hear, 'What's the matter? Did he want it too much?'

"'No,' We answered honestly. 'Not enough.'"

"'Oh my God,' Daddy said. 'You're just like me.'"

* * *

"We stayed another night with our folks and then found a room for $20.00 a week in Elgin, where we got a job as a receptionist and typist for a law firm. We liked working after the nine-year vacation. Our solitude allowed some time for healing tears. We could only eat alone, when no one shared our guilt.

"After John was assured we wouldn't immediately return to Ann Arbor, he quit his job and sold our house. We signed a quit claim deed. John moved in with his sister in Hoffman Estates about twenty miles from where we had found a room. We visited the boys every evening, but John was always present."

* * *

"Days after the separation, a young Jewish analyst explained we had the most insincere mother he had ever heard of—maybe compared to a smothering Jewish mother. Marie wasn't as bad as the therapist imagined. A third daughter's birth isn't that much to celebrate when she knew Udale was waiting for a son. Also Nancy's resulting illnesses from nearly drowning, chickenpox, and scarlet fever kept the family's lean reserves low. Her crossed eye and draining ear needed constant upkeep, meaning money which could have been used elsewhere was destined for Nancy's medical bills.

"Nevertheless, Mother's every message to us was garbled by what she knew she ought to say and what she felt. A recent survey looked at the lives of children whose mothers wanted to abort them. Mother never imagined abortion. She was Roman Catholic and it was 1940. The study followed the children for thirty odd years and found in grade school no one named them as their best friend. True of us, too. It found that at the age of twenty they had been in serious trouble. Nancy was excommunicated for marrying John. The study found that by the age of thirty they were either dead from substance abuse or seeking psychiatric care. We knew that's where we fit in as an alcoholic. We were never going to be accepted into any group of society's idea of rightness."

CHAPTER TEN
JOHNNY PEACH

April, 20, 1969
Mitchell Street House
Ann Arbor, Michigan

"Comfort and boredom, dumbfort and borecome." Johnny wondered if the meanings were synonymous for anyone else. His Buick made an automatic turn into the drive. The car might know its way home, but he never quite recognized the house as distinctly his. The buildings were slightly different in the neighborhood, an angled roof, or Tudor window, but the bit of sod and bulk of the homes were identical. The feeling that the subdivision had just violated a cornfield persisted.

Without enthusiasm he pulled himself out of the car's refuge.

A week earlier he had stayed buckled up in the closed garage for nearly an hour. When Nancy switched on the overhead light, he had been embarrassed by its invasion but somewhat vindicated. It had taken his wife that long to miss him.

"I'll have a hot cup of coffee," he called as he stepped into the spotless kitchen—no hint of supper. She hated to cook. He tried to remember what day it was and her schedule. Thursday night, usually an at-home night. He lifted his briefcase onto the table. "Where is everybody?" Not even a radio replied. He checked the bulletin board next to the phone. No clue. *Somebody's hurt*, he thought. *Maybe groceries are gone again.* He turned on the television and paged through his mail.

Then his tall neighbor was at the door. "The boys are with us."

"Bring them over. Why are they with you?"

"Seems your wife has been upset."

"What?"

"Sit down. Nancy's left you."

Johnny went to the phone, calling everyone Nancy knew. He called her folks. The neighbor and his wife brought the kids home and put them to bed. Nancy wouldn't tell her folks where she was but had agreed to see them the next morning. They were four hours away. At four o'clock in the morning, Johnny had the boys in the car heading away from the dawn.

His emotions began to roll in on him like waves—righteous anger, hurt pride, and stinging fear that he couldn't fix it this time. He panicked once when he couldn't remember her given name. He had called her Dolly for so long.

* * *

ST. CHARLES, ILLINOIS
12TH STREET HOUSE

At her folks, Marie took the boys out back to play on the sun porch.

Johnny couldn't stop talking to Udale, who merely nodded his head in response to Johnny's soliloquy. "It's beyond me. I did everything she wanted me to do. I can't believe she left me. She must be on drugs, maybe the birth-control pills. She is always after me to make more money, 'The kids need this. The kids need that.' Actually she is more a mother than a wife. She's selfish too. I know you had a hell of a time with her at home."

Udale said, "She is one of those head-strong girls, not pretty."

Marie came in for a minute to gather more cookies for the boys. "No hope chest. Just wanted a typewriter and desk."

Udale shook his head. "We thought she was going to be an old maid."

Marie stopped, before heading back to the boys. "She threw our religion in our faces to marry you."

Johnny couldn't help being who he was. "She wanted to elope. She told me your priest thought we were in trouble. I never laid a hand on her, but if she'd had her way, we would have been. I'm a Baptist believer, still am for that matter. She tried to out-Baptist me. Read the Old Testament four times and the New eight. Didn't seem to make her any happier though. I can't believe she left the kids. I could never get between them.

"For a while I was afraid she'd want to get pregnant again. Good thing she didn't. The girl was odd. Always moving the furniture around. Never satisfied with anything. I felt like I lived in a merry-go-round. The furniture went around and around the rooms. It's a good thing she couldn't move the trees. As it was, she was always clipping and shaping them. Anyway, I always provided for her. Now I'll have to quit my job and go to marriage counseling. I'll buy her a diamond. I could tell her I'll kill myself if she won't come back."

* * *

During the months that followed, Johnny wrote a short itinerary of the events:

July 23:	She called and asked me to come get her. I left immediately.
August 23:	She left again – with the kids, at her mothers.
August 25:	She filed for divorce also entered injunction against me taking the kids.
August 29:	She and I met with our attorneys trying to straighten things out – nothing doing.
September 12:	First court appearance – my witnesses testified as well as hers.
September 15:	Second court appearance – Her mother testified and the attorneys gave final arguments.
September 23:	Third court appearance – nothing happened
October 6:	Fourth court appearance – divorce awarded to me – kids awarded to me – She was very upset – I was sick.
October 10:	Fifth court appearance – my attorney and hers were there. She wasn't – The judge signed the papers – I paid.

CHAPTER ELEVEN
NANCY PEACH

Winter, Big Wolf Lake, Michigan

"SARA WILL BE THE MOST difficult to change," Betty patted Sara's knee. "Can't you recognize her stiff-necked stance a mile away?"

Rick ignored Betty's negative input. "And, Nancy, explain how you understand Sara and Betty's role in your life?"

Nancy tipped her head forward, letting her hair shield her face from view. "You don't want to say." On cue she pounded her chest. "What if you hurt their feelings?"

"We're here to search for truth." Rick's voice telegraphed his impatience. "Don't you possess enough courage and integrity to participate?"

Nancy's head went up as if Rick had slapped her back to make her burp. "Okay. Sara just hates Betty. She tries to be nice to her but she would like Betty to leave the room, if not the planet. And Betty, well she's so wrapped up in herself; she doesn't know we even exist. She studied Buddhism, you know. Don't they teach one's path should not be the only concern? Both of them take your breath away. You're afraid to voice your opinion on any subject. It's discounted anyway. You'd rather be alone to paint."

Sara touched her hair and Betty headed for the door.

"Wait," Rick said. "Tell Nancy how she's wrong."

Betty's face was red when she turned around. "Nancy is a two-timing snot. We thought we were friends when all along she's been judging our independence. Don't you know you are such a leech?"

"I don't hate anyone, Nancy." Sara's voice was way too controlled. "I love my enemies, even if they're in the same room." She stroked her throat as if to keep harsher words unsaid. "Betty, you have learned so much from talking to therapists. Maybe you should try to understand Nancy's resentment, if you can."

"That didn't go as well as I'd hoped," Rick said. "The inability to control one's anger is a symptom of many psychological problems. Truth can be painful but brutality is not called for."

"Sorry," Nancy started to weep. "You told him." She coughed on the next words. "Now they won't ever include you."

Rick controlled a revealing smile. "I promise you, Nancy, the three of you will be closer than ever. Let's try this. Without speaking tell yourself how the feedback from your friends alters your inner thoughts."

Betty's frown suggested all the news was not comforting. Nancy's tears were unabated while Sara hugged herself more tightly.

"I promise your worse fears will come to nothing," Rick said. "We will find a viable option for all of you to live with. Do any of you want to share what you've learned thus far?"

"My judgments aren't worthy of me," Sara said.

"Even the perception of myself. I know the Lord loves me, faults and all. And my friends are included and forgiven by His presence in the world and by His saving death and resurrection." She went on, "Betty presents a false identity even to herself. I think you see through her defenses all the way to her true identity."

Rick nodded and Sara continued, "Nancy's self-hatred could be cured with a compassionate regime. Nancy, every time you start to ruminate about doubting your talent, you should stop and start something you enjoy—even making a milk shake. When your soul is quieter, go back and find the inciting incident which caused the negative onslaught. I think you'll find some outlandish, unattainable goal slapped you down. The entire world doesn't need to bow and scrape before you. Your work is appreciated by a subjective audience. If you add humility enhancement to your thought agenda, your true essence will surprise you with self-confidence and an easier way of accepting the reality of those around you."

Rick reassured himself. Sara was the guiding light of these three friends. He trusted her even more to handle his solutions with grace and stamina. "Have you used Rubin's tools successfully?"

Sara laughed. "Caught me. Yes, his 'Compassion and Self-Hatred' worked on me. I discovered I do treat rich people differently than poor people. I admitted to myself that I'm demanding and need someone to rely on."

"I'm as suicidal as a rat in a foodless maze." Betty admitted. "Are we strong enough to tolerate much more truth?"

Rick moved from his pillowed position to the couch next to Betty. "We won't let anything happen to you."

Nancy pushed him away from her. "He just used the

word brutal for the words you said to each other. And once said, words can't be swallowed."

"There's truth in your statement." Rick slipped his arm up on the back of the couch and tapped her shoulder. "You have found new courage, right?"

Nancy drew her hair behind her ears. "Yep, but just what happens next?"

"Aye, there's the rub," Sara said. "I believe in magic, but what if I don't fit into your idea of who I am."

"While I put the food trays in the hall," Rick instructed softly, "could you all move the coffee table to the middle of the room?" When he returned from his chore, Rick moved pillows around the low table to accommodate the group. As he sat on the pillow nearest the door, he said. "Finger tips on the table, please."

"Good heavens," Nancy said. "Are you just going to levitate it?"

"I hope not," Rick said. "I'd be as surprised as you. Now close your eyes and concentrate on each breath."

Silence filled the room.

Rick coached them. "Keep meditating on your breath. Count one on the first breath out, two on the next—up to four, then start over with one. When your thoughts stray, don't yank your mind back to the task. Bring it slowly back into line as you would a child or a horse you love. We'll try this for fifteen minutes to see if we can quiet your minds." Rick checked to see if their eyes were closed.

The grandfather clock chimed 5:30 p.m. Shadows were deepening around the room. The flickering candles allowed mysterious shapes to float and wane along the walls.

Nancy asked, "Shall you tell him what you're thinking about or just what you envision?"

Here was progress. She trusted him enough to share. "Of course, but keep your eyes closed," was all he said, making sure he didn't intimidate her landscape of self-realizations.

"You see Gauguin sitting in his hut in Tahiti. His paints are spread out almost in a rainbow around him. He's dabbing samples of each onto his palette. A blank canvass is propped up against a wall made of interwoven sticks and branches. He's watching three women on a red blanket, resting in the sunshine just outside the hut's small entrance. They seem unaware that he's inspecting their movements. Or maybe they're accustomed to being subjects for his paintings. First, he stands and outlines them with broad black strokes." Nancy opened her eyes. "You're losing him. Bring him back."

"Close your eyes and wait," Rick directed.

Nancy didn't speak, but she inclined her head as if listening to someone.

Rick tried to keep his curiosity under control. Forbearance had never been a familiar quality of his. Finally he said, "Anything, Nancy?"

"No," she said, keeping her eyes closed. "Wait for you."

Rick squirmed. Hadn't he waited long enough? The hands on the clock were inching toward 6:00.

Nancy raised her left hand. "You just can't follow."

Sara jumped into the fray. "Let them go, Nancy. We're here for you."

Nancy shook her head. "But they know how you feel.'

"What do you feel?" Betty asked.

"If you can just learn by copying their examples," Nancy voice was almost a whisper. She was on her knees. "What worth are you?"

Rick said. "That's not what they told you. Who spoke the most?"

"Mother." Nancy started to rise but then stayed on her knees. "She was in the hut with Gauguin, asking him about you."

"Even that's progress, isn't it Rick?" Sara moved onto her pillow. "I mean Mr. Fitzgerald."

"We're going to get pretty intimate here. You might just as well keep calling me Rick."

"Answer her," Betty's voice rumbled with irritation

"Tolerance," Rick said then laughed at himself. "Do tell us, Nancy."

"Gauguin told Mother he was never accepted as a talented artist until after his death. Mother said you probably wouldn't be happy with that scenario. He just laughed at her. 'Make sure she keeps at it,' he said. 'No harm will come to her. She will appreciate the beauty of the world more, even if her renditions lack credulity to others.'" Nancy giggled. "Is that good enough?"

Rick reached across the table to touch Nancy's cheek. "Were Gauguin's words good enough for you to let go of your inhibitions?"

Nancy opened her eyes and nodded. "You don't know if you told him, whenever you get in the car to paint at the City Club, you pull down the visor to check your wig—and you're always smiling."

"You enjoy painting," Sara said.

Nancy smiled broadly. "It's like it's time to play. When you smear bright colors on your canvases, you don't need to worry about your boys' struggles, your husband's health, or even the world's problems. You love it! You don't need anyone's acclaim for your efforts. You're happy painting, blissfully so."

Rick tapped the table. "You will never need to stop painting in your lifetime."

"I guess that's true." Nancy spread her hands on the table as if reconsidering the worth of her fingers.

Betty broke in, "Does this mean you'll stop complaining and just paint?"

Nancy answered the challenge. "You promise, you'll only hear from you when you're not allowed enough time or freedom to paint. You want to finish a painting once you start it. Sara and Betty both drain so much energy."

Nancy pointed at Rick. "Listening to them and understanding what's being said behind their words, Rick is able to tap into their wordless intense worlds, too." Nancy tapped her bosom. "You respect Sara's writing time and you did accept Betty's schedule of sexual exploits. Maybe you were too accepting. But you loved seeing Betty doll herself up to be attractive even at her age. Sara's outlook gets rosy after she's able to slip into her fictional writing world. Why can't they understand you? Where's the unity of our friendship? They see you as a flighty failure because you don't want to sign or sell your work, whereas you take pride in the production. Betty disappoints you by ignoring your output. Sara's need to control squashes your ideas. Stops your paint brushes."

"We can make sure your schedule is secure," Sara promised.

Rick congratulated himself on the progress of the group as well as its increasing cohesiveness. "Betty, what did you see while your eyes were closed?"

Betty shook her head. "Do you want to hear about our bedroom antics?"

"Keep it clean," Sara said. "You need to get closure for your resentments against men."

"Couldn't have said it better," Rick said. "I know the courage required to open up in front of a stranger."

Betty reared back then clasped her fingers on the table. "Better hold onto something. How many lovers do you think we've had?"

"Does it matter to you?" Rick asked.

"In a way. Will anyone ever love us? We justified our promiscuous phase as a need to prove we were attractive to men, after our first husband left us to live with a younger man." Betty laughed then covered her mouth. "We like laughter. It settles our stomach. Did you know men don't appreciate laughter during love making, no matter how good the joke is?"

Rick shook his head.

Betty went on, "Off the subject of men or maybe because of the number, our moods fluctuate daily. The variation tempos are faster and faster with extremes on both ends: highs to lows then back to highs. We feel as if we're on a perpetual roller coaster, barely hanging on with a trembling grip. It's exhausting." Betty unclasped her fingers and held up her shaking hands. "See what you've done to us. Do you want us to leave here unhinged?"

"You are in the safest environment you could find on this earth." Rick held out his hands and Betty grasped them. "How did you survive?" Rick asked. "That was a dangerous phase of your life."

All three women nodded.

Betty let go of Rick's safety line. "When Mother was dying, we visited her for about two weeks. We told her we knew she had to be praying for us throughout the years or we would have been injured or killed. Mother said she'd never stopped including us in her prayers. Do you believe I miss her?"

"You'd be a stone if you didn't miss Mother." Sara was still clutching her arms as if to hold onto herself.

Betty sobered. "Are you able to alleviate such humiliating choices in the future?"

"If you're up to the challenge." Then Rick asked, "What's the most adventurous thing you did?"

Betty relaxed and laughed a little. "When we didn't want one lover to leave, we actually laid down in the snow in front of his car!"

"Wow." Rick shifted his legs, which he thought were falling asleep. Betty had *not* asked a question for once!

"And we got pretty close to connecting with the mob." Betty spoke rapidly as if realizing he was getting restless, "We'll give you the details later. One time a Native-American giant grabbed the back of our hair in a bar. He asked us if we needed food stamps or other help. We'd just sold him a school bus we bought for another man to go hunting. When, gee whiz, I forgot his name. When the big guy left, the bartender told us his hand was on the gun under the bar in case the guy got any rougher."

Betty raced her words together to keep Rick's interest. "That same day, one of the guy's friends from the reservation near Rockford challenged us to take a ride on his motorcycle. Of course we didn't wear helmets back then. Too crazy to be careful. Anyway, there we were driving too fast down the center line of a two-lane highway, passing cars while oncoming traffic honked nearly brushing us as they passed on the other side of the road. We hung onto the pipsqueak for dear life. We remember thinking, *If we die you're coming with us.*"

"How many years did you ...?" Sara blushed.

Betty laughed. "We stopped when we started marrying people instead of dating them. We'd quit drinking for a while too. We knew we used men the same way and for the same reasons we reached for our next drink. Our lives were a mess and we couldn't face it."

"Did the therapy help?" Sara asked.

"We used them as confessors. That's Catholic upbringing for you."

Sara tapped her ring on the coffee table. "When I was about ten, standing in line for confession, I went through the ten commandments. I'd memorized them. The only word I didn't recognize was 'adultery.' So I told the priest, I'd committed adultery. At least I didn't hear him laugh, but I received five Our Fathers and an entire rosary for penance."

Betty stuttered. "No, no penances were meted out. The therapists listened. Maybe that's all we needed." Betty was quiet for a while as if rehearsing her words before speaking again. "The mob almost got involved. We knew quite a few members. One time we were complaining about work, some injustice from the boss or straw boss. Our listener asked if we wanted any help dealing with him. We caught on pretty fast. One act of theirs would have required us to reciprocate when the mob wanted help. At least we had the sense to decline his offer."

Betty stood up and flexed her arms. Then she picked up her purse.

Rick stood too, thinking she might want to leave too soon.

Instead Betty fished in her purse for a hair brush, which Nancy appropriated. Nancy dipped her head to her knees, letting her long brown hair fall nearly to the floor. She brushed her head of hair from the base of her neck over her head to the ends in front of her. Then she whipped her head back allowing the spray of hair to fall down her back.

Sara tsk'd. "I suppose you two think that's sexy."

Rick sat back down motioning for the three of them to resume their seats on the pillows. "I don't think Betty has finished her story."

So Betty arched her back, putting her elbows on the low table. "We didn't marry for ten years between the second and third marriages. But when men ask us to marry them and we tell them no, they don't want to be friends anymore."

"You found that surprising?" Rick asked.

"We understand now," Betty said. "At the time though, it was confusing and disappointing. At one point, a talented man we admired asked us to marry him. He was in the middle of fighting for custody of his two boys. We had watched Nancy suffer through those changes, so we gave our standard negative answer. Of course he stopped wasting his time with us. We promised ourselves the next decent man who proposed would not be rejected. That was our third husband. Another mistake."

"How so," Rick asked.

"Well, we'd been lovers for about two years, away from home, because the boys were teenagers. However, it gets pretty uncomfortable in the winter, going out into the freezing night from a warm bed. We hadn't met his friends or family. So we called him on it. He arranged for us to meet his folks. His mother was a case. We sat in the living room with his quiet father but we could hear his fish-wife carry on in the kitchen with her only son. They were arguing loudly about something. His father noticed our distress and said, 'You know sometimes you should get a divorce, but it doesn't seem worth it.'"

Rick nodded. "Go on. What was wrong with the guy? Why did you finally divorce?"

Betty laughed. "I remember during the divorce my lawyer said he couldn't understand it. Who paid for what, who cooked? The judge tried to give us our ex's car. We made sure not to accept it or any alimony. Hey, you didn't ask about our second husband?"

"You haven't told us what went wrong with this third marriage."

"Complicated," Betty sighed. "The bottom line was when Nancy's boys both went off to college and we were attending the community college on Saturdays, we'd told him to be in bed when we got home in the afternoon. He wasn't. So we fought about it. We asked him what was so wrong with asking your husband to make love."

"He said, 'Let me think of something you would loathe.'"

Rick couldn't help sucking in his breath with shock.

"Yep," Betty said. "We drove around trying to find another place to live. We threw the wedding ring out the car window. That week he was scheduled to go on an out-of-town business trip to a convention of some sort. As soon as he was gone on Monday, we called in sick and started packing up."

Betty threw her purse across the room. "Nancy's boys never understood, even after we told them what he had said."

Sara patted Betty's shoulder. "Not much luck with men."

"So, do you want to hear about number two?"

"Sure," Rick said.

"We'll keep it short. When the judge asked us why we wanted the divorce, we told him. We were reading feminist books in the guest bedroom, which we used when Nancy's boys visited. John fought for custody to get Nancy to go back to him."

"Wait a minute." Rick waved his arm to get her attention. "Stay with the second husband story, then we'll get back to Nancy." Rick looked at the clock, 5:50. "Go ahead. That's why we're here—to free you from the bitterness you are carrying around, dragging you down with the weight of resentments."

"Okay," Betty said. "Anyway we were reading an interesting book about the history of women's rights and Ken kept coming in asking us to help him watch—I think a football game was on television. We kept telling him no. We wanted to read. All of a sudden we heard this thudding sound in the front room. We laid down the book and went in to see what the racket was. He was laying belly-down on the rug, kicking his hands and feet—a temper tantrum."

"'Divorce granted,' the judge said. He banged his gavel, too."

Betty slid her right arm out and Sara grabbed it. "It's too hard for her," Sara said. "Being angry and resentful is like drinking poison and hoping the other person will die."

Nancy peeked around Sara shoulder. "Let her tell it, before she just gives up completely."

Betty said, "We tried to reconcile. Nancy missed her boys. John even bought us a diamond ring. Our own mother, Marie, said he was faking it. His brother-in-law laughed when he was telling us about my husband bragging. John had lied to us about wanting to commit suicide, to get us back."

"There's more," Sara prompted her.

"When we left Ken, our second husband, we didn't get a divorce for two years. Instead, Mrs. Mac, the housekeeper for Nancy's boys told us she'd arranged with John for us to come back as her replacement housekeeper. Nancy's would have a chance to be with her boys. There wasn't anything we wouldn't have done to help her live with them. So we prostituted ourselves with their father."

Sara said, "I helped her out by writing a book, telling Nancy's side of the marriage. That was when Betty returned to John while she was married to her second husband, Ken—just to be with Nancy's boys. When John read it, he promised Nancy would get the boys if they couldn't make the marriage work."

Betty laughed. "You can imagine. The poor man wanted us to divorce our second husband to remarry him, but we knew what the courts would say. He was living with a married women—not someone a judge would declare fit to raise Nancy's boys. He never received another kind word from us. That's when he left to live with a younger man. And then our second husband, Ken, wanted to marry another woman, who had the same birthday as us. We went back to Michigan and got a divorce for . . ." Betty laughed again, "or from him."

Rick tried to gain some control of the conversation's direction. "When you closed your eyes at the beginning of the session, what did you see?"

Betty smirked. "We saw the coat tree where we hung a pair of men's pants and prayed to Saint Ann to find us a man with integrity."

"I found Powell," Sara said.

CHAPTER THIRTEEN
RICK FITZGERALD

RICK WISHED HE'D RECORDED the session or at least taken more notes. The women led interesting, complicated lives—especially Betty. Between them he counted four husbands with two of them intermittently sharing Nancy's two sons. One of them mentioned Nancy's boys, who were both married. One lived near Seattle and the other was near Tucson, according to Tanya.

"Sara, it's your turn," Rick said.

Sara gripped her hands. "I hope I remember everything from the meditation. Hemmingway admitted he was a blood-crazed veteran unable to deal with the deaths he'd personally caused. He stank of booze and something worse, maybe he was ill. It was hot in Cuba and the humid air wasn't moving. We sat in wicker chairs. He was drinking something dark brown. It wasn't the ice tea his skinny wife or maid had served me. Hemmingway towered over me even sitting in his chair. He leaned forward, repeating again and again, 'Tell the truth for all its worth.' On the other side of me in a white rocking chair, Mark Twain kept pulling on his white vest. I explained to him how I appreciated his effort to capture the nature of humankind. Between puffs of cigar smoke he said, 'Keep at it until you know it's right.'"

"It's six o'clock," Rick said. "Do you think we're making progress?"

Betty shook her head. "Sara, you need to tell him about Robert Koelz."

"Is there time?" Sara asked.

Rick stroked his chin, wondering how he was going to conceal his plans for the rest of the session without lying to them. "We're going to stay at this until all three of you are satisfied with the results. I can promise you won't leave this room until you agree."

"Okay," Sara said. "I met a bookstore owner named Robert Koelz when I first lived in Ann Arbor. I called him to ask him about the value of some old books I'd collected. One was on bicycling." She wiped her forehead. "Better relax, Rick, this is a long story."

Sara Powell

Sara wondered where to start. The bookman became such an important part of her life. "He fathered me," she said. "My first husband had convinced me I was stupid. It's ironic because I was impressed when he read me Plato's *The Cave*."

Rick nodded. "The man chained to a wall saw shadows from the entrance on the opposite wall."

"And thought that was reality," Sara finished. "John used the book to convince me to open my mind about the Roman Catholic faith. He never read another book all the time I knew him that wasn't strictly technical. No biographies, no fiction, nothing. But he was intelligent. His father was an inventor for General Electric, I think.

"Anyway after nine years of marriage to this uneducated son of a genius, my conversations ended or started with equivocations. 'Maybe, I don't really know, perhaps, but I'm stupid . . .' Sometimes if even *I* thought I was getting redundant, I would add that my father hadn't completed eighth grade, but had answers for everything. I learned a lot of wrong things. I guess you could call them suppositions."

She checked Rick's reaction. He was listening intently. How could she gauge if she'd impressed him about Robert's significance? "After I had gotten to know Koelz, he stopped me in my tracks when I started every statement with 'maybe' or 'probably.'"

"'You're not stupid,' Robert said. 'You're just not formally educated.'"

"As my Jewish husband says, 'Who knew'?" Sara laughed and Rick joined in.

"When did you and the bookman become friends?" Rick asked.

"During Nancy's divorce," Sara said. "I called Robert every day. When I quit the job I'd taken during the Illinois divorce, my entire salary was taken to pay off the long-distance calls I'd made to Jackson, Michigan. I also counted on Robert to justify my new political alliance with the Democrats. When I had watched the Chicago convention riots, I saw a burly policeman shove a white woman into a plate-glass window. She was wearing white gloves and clutching her purse. John said the woman must have been swearing at the policeman. She didn't seem capable of mouthing the word *damn*."

Rick nodded but didn't interrupt.

"Back then department stores would hem a man's pants for free—but not a woman's. I once was told after a successful job interview in Jackson, that I'd been hired because of my beautiful legs. They never saw them again. I wore pants on the job for seven years."

Nancy laughed. "Despite that, she found Betty's third husband there, right?"

Betty said, "He told us the first time we worked for the architecture firm, he'd wanted to date us. And, he wasn't going to let us get away again."

Sara smiled. "But I want to tell you how close I became to Robert Koelz. In November of 1969, I moved to Jackson after Nancy divorced. Koelz found me a room in a boarding house. I worked as a temp for the utility company, until I found permanent employment with a felt-cutting plant."

"Where we met our second husband, Ken." Betty smiled ear-to-ear with the added information. "Tell him about the government contracts."

Sara frowned, irritated with the changes in subjects. "During the Viet Nam War, I tried to find employment that wasn't defense oriented. Felt manufacturing seemed harmless enough until I learned they made the plugs for bullets. I was hired as the purchasing manager's secretary. When the government contracts arrived from Washington, I threw them in the waste basket. No one ever found out, but I bet their income suffered."

Rick scratched his head. "I would keep that account secret. I don't know how long the statute of limitations lasts for a Federal crime."

"Hey," Betty boomed. "Didn't you to want tell about Robert bombing the recruiting station in Jackson?"

"Never happened," Rick said. "Let's move to the couch. We'll all be more comfortable."

"He's not going to believe my story," Sara said.

"Tell him anyway," Nancy chorused in harmony with Betty.

After they moved from the pillows to the couch, Rick said, "Go ahead. I'd like to hear about the bombings."

"You're right, the recruiting station was never bombed," Sara sighed. "During the Viet Nam war, Robert's bulletin board was filled with dreadful death statistics. Molly Savage, her brother and a few other radicals, whom Robert had encouraged, decided to bomb the recruiting station which was about eight blocks from the bookstore. I told Robert to telephone them to call off the violence—because, I'd be standing in front of the building. He convinced them I had nothing to lose and was crazy enough to stop them."

Rick hands were in his hair. "You still think Robert was a friend of yours?"

Sara nodded her head. "Robert fell in love with me while I was still in Illinois. He wrote me a letter comprised entirely of my name, 'Sara, Sara, I think of Sara, Sara'—a full page of 'Sara' changing to red ink at times."

"Customers to the bookshop arrived up a flight of stairs, down an echoing hall to the opened door. Usually they would stop to read the newest radical postings on the hall's bulletin board before entering. The subjects became the topics of the day's conversations. Robert's cluttered desk was set diagonally facing the entrance. Two smaller bookcases framed a closed door to his living quarters. Five unmatched chairs and cardboard boxes filled with books welcomed visitors to stay a while."

"Robert smoked constantly, rocking in his squeaky desk chair. His right arm rested over the rotary dial telephone. He often wore a blue linen shirt with a blue-and-gold paisley cravat. His slacks were grey wool, his shoes always shined. He was quick to point out his hair and mustache provided him some resemblance to Mark Twain."

"Among his friends, Henry was about the same age, fifty-two, but he was thicker and slightly balding. He was the painter of the pictures on the bookshop's far wall. One was all bright coral-rose of a reclining nude, supposedly his wife's portrait. The one I bought was of Lake Superior where the beach was filled with stones not yet turned to sand. Henry usually sat at the drop-leaf desk."

"On one visit I wore a short black, furry coat which I would dramatically throw at a chair. My long-sleeved red-and-gold paisley dress was fingertip length and my black, knee-high, laced boots didn't hide fine legs. I wore glasses then and my shyness forced me to be aggressive. I remember saying, 'I'm a fellow citizen.'"

"To which Robert replied, 'Well the town's been going downhill.'"

"In response to his teasing, I often thumped him on his chest, saying, 'Die, fool.' When he died, I remembered the foreshadowing."

"'Ruffian,' Robert would scream, hugging me. 'Haven't you read *Through the Looking Glass*? Alice was always polite.'"

"I rambled on and on when I was with him, not needing to censure my thoughts. I told him I hated the word 'nice' because it falsely guaranteed happiness if I kept quiet. It was a decree of murder, a self-imposed death. Just be a good geisha and shut up. I told him about a stuffed parrot attached to the passenger seat of a car. Too appropriate. All the driver needed was someone to repeat his favorite philosophy. As long as I'm alive, I'm going to be heard from—even if they hate me. Even if I'm alone the rest of my life. How's that for raw courage?

"Once when I was seventeen, babysitting for my sister Jean, Daddy promised to drive me home. The three of us were only teenagers—three years apart. When my sister and her husband came home we chatted away. I finally remembered to look out the window for Daddy and there he was in his Oldsmobile. When I got in the car I asked him why he hadn't come up to the door and knocked to let us know he'd arrived. He backhanded me across my face, slamming my glasses against my nose.

"I didn't speak to Daddy for an entire year. I was the only one still living at home. Both my sisters were married and my younger brother was in the seminary trying to be a priest in order to send the entire family to heaven. Mother, Daddy, and I had previously carried on long conversations. I wasn't afraid to argue with him or tell him when he was wrong. After a year of my complete silence, he gave me a watch for Christmas, telling Mother, I had improved. Had all my previous conversations with him been static—not worth the time to listen?

"And another time, after Nancy's initial separation from John, she had returned for two months. I tried to convince him she'd changed into a progressive woman sure of her intelligence—instead of a doormat. It was a useless endeavor. Nancy shut up for two days. No word of dissention, no contradictions. John said he thought they could get along because Nancy was improving. If she entirely erased who she was, John was happy!

"Her life had belonged to her parents and then to her husband. The marriage, house, religion, and friends belonged to someone else. I wanted it all back. As long as I am alive I'm going to be heard from."

"How did Koelz react to your freedom manifesto?" Rick asked.

"Robert called me an anti-social witchlet, worse a 'mud turtle.' I had told him about John's spies. How he was always threatening and distrustful. John thought I would kidnap Nancy's boys for her. He didn't even know I wouldn't break any law because I prize freedom above anything else.

"Sherry was Robert's favorite drink and became mine, too. Robert often pontificated, 'Marriage is without merit. One has not the liberty to call on old friends or relatives. Your hands and feet seem tied. If you want to go out, you are asked why, and if you don't you are gradually estranged from your friends. Besides being a bargain to which only the entrance is free, its continuance being constrained and forced, depending otherwise than on our will, and a bargain ordinarily made for other ends, there supervene a thousand foreign tangles to unravel, enough to break the thread and trouble the course of a lively affection, according to Montaigne.'"

"When I came back to Robert after Betty's second marriage, sixteen year old Molly and her brother Mike also visited the book shop. Mike wore a blue navy raincoat that was as long as he was tall. His full beard reached his chest and his black hair covered both shoulders. He would sit silently with arms crossed. Molly, the blonde bright-eyed hippie wore a jacket with a white neck scarf swinging past her tight jeaned knees. I didn't appreciate her sitting on Robert's lap with her arm around his neck. Mike would fish out money for the books she wanted.

"To get Robert's attention, I would detail the progress of Nancy's fight for her sons. Nancy told me her oldest son, at age seven, was getting confused and a little frightened— although Carl told Nancy he knew she'd come home soon. About five, Tom the baby told Nancy his aunt's house was messy but mostly he just sat on her lap and meowed like a lost kitten.

"After my move to Jackson the end of May 1969, I lived in a furnished apartment near Sparton Electronics where I worked as the personnel secretary. Before my first paycheck came, I only had five dollars, some food and dirty laundry. I figured the food wouldn't last long enough, so I hand laundered even the sheets with dish soap on the corduroy ribbed drain board of the sink. It was the cleanest wash I'd ever seen—Tide or not.

"Robert also introduced me to a twenty-mile, meandering forest preserve called Waterloo. The Michigan farmers had sold unusable property to the State to cover taxes during the Depression. For me, the wooded hills, lakes, bogs, and rolling meadows replaced the harmony invoking rituals of fleeing as a child to the Illinois pasture behind the Rossmoor farm. Painful realities of not being loved enough disappeared as I drove towards the woods.

"When I knew Robert, I'd lost my faith. The universe didn't seem to give a damn. All was vanity. Nothing mattered. I was convinced marriage was a string of socially-cemented, stale days. All criticism, love and indifference were provided by a one-member human race. Nancy's husband wouldn't let her work or go back to school.

"Robert knew the habits of the free creatures in the woods. My favorite story was of the yellow finches, who couldn't sing and fly at the same time. A bird would take off, flying straight up until it got so excited that it would sing and promptly fall about eight inches. The finch would resume its mad flapping to gain altitude to once again break into grateful song, whereupon it would plummet down again. We laughed at the poor thing's antics.

"But I missed Nancy's boys. I would turn away from

children in the streets, surprised at the force and power of overwhelming grief. Many nights were spent crying myself into a state of exhaustion.

"Once a kitten was left on my doorstep to help with the loneliness. The cat was climbing out of its box, meowing for food. After she was fed, the little tyke began washing its face furiously, finally using both paws and falling over in the process. She looked so cute and helpless; I dubbed her 'Sweets.' While I was at work, she would leave broken crockery and footprints as evidence of her dashing exploits. Sweets would lie in my hair at night with her paw on my eye or mouth.

"I read continuously. John treated reading as a nasty habit. He accused Nancy of getting sexually aroused by the books. Sweets didn't appreciate the lack of attention either. She would run upside down along the bottom of the couch where I was reading, then over my feet, body, book, and face. Disconcerting, but endearing.

"Robert's entertaining imagination held few constraints. Even sober, he conversed freely with his cat, Miss Poi, even if she was out of sight. I felt I had lived upon dumplings instead of carrots. Life was raw, upright and noisy. Robert explained I had never been loved by my parents or husband and didn't even know how to love. My motivation to justify any satisfaction began to fade. Running away from Nancy's marriage left the problems on hold. I couldn't reconcile my need to see Nancy's boys, which I felt to my bones. Nails under the comfortable mattress, my sorrow was like a toothache no painkiller could reach."

Sara produced an index card from her purse. "I don't want to change a word of Kahil Gibran." Then she read, "'Unhappy is the man who loves a maiden and takes her for his life mate, pouring out at her feet the sweat of his brow and his heart's blood, placing in her hands the fruits of his labor and yield of his toil, and then learns, suddenly, that her heart, which he sought to buy with exertion by day and watchfulness by night, is given as a gift to another that he may take pleasure in its hidden things and rejoice in the secrets of its love. Unhappy the woman who awakens from youth's ignorance to find herself in the house of a man who overwhelms her with his gifts and riches and clothes her with generosity and kindliness, yet is not able to touch her heart with the living flame of love nor yet satisfy her spirit with the divine wine that God makes to flow from a man's eyes into a woman's heart.'"

Rick asked, "And who was this 'other' partaking in the secrets of your heart?"

"Nancy's two sons and, platonically, I suppose, Robert Koelz, the bookman."

Betty interrupted. "Nancy left to stay alive; she'd lost seven pounds and found her mind settled on suicide possibilities every day. Nancy's boys needed her to survive."

"Absolutely," Rick agreed.

Sara continued, "When I mentioned suicide to Robert, he shared the story of his older brother's success at the deed after he found there wasn't enough money during the Great Depression to send him to college. Robert was a lifeline to me, someone to hold onto while everything was being thrown overboard. I also noticed a budding egotism, convinced I had conquered an obviously intelligent man, a bookman.

"Robert asked me when I first noticed my unhappiness. I told him it came like a gentle tide lapping playfully at my toes, a tear here, a sob there. And as relentless as the tide, it stormed my knees, collapsed me, overwhelming me with waves of despair. I told him I was raised a Catholic and converted to Bible Fundamentalism when Nancy married her Baptist husband. I even searched the scriptures for an answer from God. Every night I would go to bed alone with my doubts alleviated by the holy words. But each morning would bring ten new questions or contradictions to be countered.

"Finally, Robert's aura of perfection slipped. After being asked to dine on duck at a Chinese restaurant with Robert's friends, I was given the check to pay. Robert's grin lost some of its brilliance. He flaunted me before his stodgy friends. With books, he believed in keeping the product scarce and the market ready. He supposed his friends would provide for him. Henry ran a cleaning shop and arranged for Robert's cleaning tab to be processed without charge. Another friend paid the bookshop rent, others made sure they bought enough books to keep him fed.

"During the first two months I visited Nancy's boys whenever I could afford the gas money. I asked to come home. When I did go home, John threatened in any argument to disappear with Nancy's children. In order to stop him with a court order, Nancy needed a divorce. He wasn't ready to be embarrassed by a divorce so he schemed to wrestle the children away. He paid relatives and neighbors to testify about Nancy's incompetence, yet asked her to come back at every opportunity. He knew the only way she would stay with him would be to secure custody of the boys. So he sought, or bought, custody and won—for eighteen months.

"I stayed alone with Mother and Daddy until my brother-in-law attempted to rape me. My mother didn't believe me. When my parents left for Florida, Mother gave her keys to the same brother-in-law. I remember asking Robert how two four-limbed people could be meshed for life, other than in a pushme-pushyou hate-alliance. Surely it is some relic of a barbarous age. I recall some of the more poetic lines of the letter I wrote him, 'If you would like my few hours of this short life, if screaming, clowning, and breathing are allowed, I'll sit by your fire and happily spin yellow-straw days from one grey-quiet hour. Purple tulips will I conjure from fingernails and black dirt. I will knead wholesome bread and sun air clean. I will feed cat and properly bow and scrape whilst doing so. I will show reverence only to books. I shall love you, if you like. But if you are unable to swallow such a stone-studded remedy, then I will pack up my black bag of me and trundle off to someone else's sunny bed. Fresh from the Barbarian Horde, I come. Can you unmuck me enough to serve any useful purpose?'"

Rick appeared impressed. "You memorized your letter."

"Yep," Sara said. "Why are you surprised? Once I woke in the morning with an entire poem in my head, 'Why sleepeth thou whilst heavens quake, beyond the mortal sea? Prepare to tear the cosmic screen, serene.'"

"Exactly what I intend to do for you all," Rick smiled. "We need to move on. It's 6:30."

CHAPTER FOURTEEN
RICK FITZGERALD

THE THREE FRIENDS NEEDED to be prepared. Rick rehearsed how he might broach the subject of their transformation. 'All for one,' came to mind. He smiled. "Sara, have you finished your tale of Robert's effect on your life?"

"Hardly," Nancy said.

"Just getting started." Betty's ornery laugh filled the room.

Sara's face was serious. "I couldn't last long alone without Nancy's boys. Betty married Ken in May of 1970. He refused to let me visit Robert. Robert Koelz had been the song in my heart, kindled the flame in my eyes, and is even now the remembered spice in my life."

Sara inspected the ends of her hair. "No split ends now. But there were times when Robert quoted entire passages of Hemmingway's novels with Robert himself as the lead character. He said he was the man that jumped over the wall to find a dead gray-haired man. And he was the sad soldier searching the man's pockets only to find pictures of the wife and child. But, in the nine months I knew him, I spoke more than I had in nine years in the marriage I had endured. When Koelz learned Betty's second husband Ken wouldn't allow me to visit him, he wrote me a note, 'A Gospel of Love according to you; Where love is not, you return unbidden; Where love is, you stay away.'"

"Not quite two years after Betty married Ken, she left him to be with Nancy's boys and John. I remember one drinking party which ended in another bed scene with the boys' father and Betty. She was surprised to not feel anything. No excitement, no arousal, just indestructibility. I called Robert and we discussed at least divorcing Ken. But divorcing Ken meant there would be no grounds to plead for custody of the children. I was glad Betty had taken over the bed scenes. The act was legalized prostitution for Betty to gain Nancy time with her boys."

Sara rubbed her forehead. "Robert and I told each other we were in love, past the need to be daily together, past the time of total acceptance of each other. Later that same evening, when I was again in a haze of alcohol, Robert's friends called me, one after another, to prove it was true. Robert died of a stroke that awful night.

"I was never bored while Robert lived. Even when we were apart it was as if his audience added meaning to my life. Thank the Lord, I finally stopped drinking and rekindled my faith in a personal creator aware of each twitch of my eyelid."

Rick was still listening. "When did you stop drinking?"

"Not even how?" Nancy asked.

"It was legalizing the breath test, right?" Betty's voice dropped with the seriousness of the subject.

"The boys were both in college. Betty had left her third husband." Sara sighed. "I was stopped by the police a final time in 1983 with a half cup of sherry in the console of my red 1965 Mustang. I quickly put fresh lilies-of-the-valley in the shoulder of my sweater nearest the door. I took off my sunglasses and shut off the radio. When I answered the state trooper's questions, I would turn my head away telling him how concerned I was about the right front tire's alignment. He had stopped me because I'd been weaving all over the road. He let me go with a warning to fix my car—without a ticket. I realized I didn't want to call the boys to come bail me out of jail for drunk driving."

"Your last drinking spree was a dilly," Nancy said.

Rick cocked his head. "Your?"

"We often drank together," Betty said. "Why don't I remember getting stopped in the Mustang?"

"You didn't come along that time," Sara said. "But the last time in 1983, we ended up driving down a two-lane highway, Route 127, to my home in Clark Lake. Earlier in that particular tavern, a man sitting across the room was smiling at me. I recognized him as the wife beater of a friend of mine, so I raised my fist at him with my thumb pointed down, as if I were Caesar determining the fate of a gladiator. I even mouthed, 'Die sucker!' I heard he later ran his car into a tree and killed himself. On that nightmarish night, I kept waking up in the oncoming lane of Route 127 from cars honking at me. It never occurred to me to stop the car to sleep it off."

"You're lucky you weren't killed!" Rick crossed his arms.

"I was more lucky that I didn't kill anyone." Sara brushed her hair behind her shoulders. "I had a part-time job on Saturdays. Most alcoholics are work-alcoholics, too. I worked for a lawyer in Jackson. I was late for work that morning and explained I still felt a bit tipsy. He asked me if I had a problem, so I related the night's dangerous escapade. The lawyer took me to my first Alcoholics Anonymous meeting. I didn't know he had a problem with alcohol. I attended meetings by myself a few times. I was still an atheist at the time and figured the program was a God-thing. They did give me an answer about why I kept drinking when I didn't want to. I was allergic to alcohol. Once I took one sip I kept drinking until I passed out. So I stopped taking the first drink.

"I remember sharing with Betty that they also said there were some people who were constitutionally incapable of complete honesty. They were born that way. She told me later she had cleared up a lot of complications in her life, I assumed with married men, simply by deciding not to lie to anyone any more. After all, the wives were being lied to.

"Later I was brought to my knees by the abundance the Lord rained down on me. Did I tell you I was out of work for four months one time? I needed the job to continue a Bachelor Program at Eastern Michigan University for life-work credit. Out of the blue I received a scholarship, a car filled with gas to look for a job, and a job. I went to my knees and thanked the universe, renewing my belief in my personal Savior. I was so familiar with privation, the only way the Lord could reach me was by His lavish abundance.

"I concluded Jesus had to be in heaven before he figured out the answer to the wine-bibbers that He'd hung around with while on earth. So, He inspired my friend Bill, the founder of AA, with the answer. I didn't go to meetings, never read the Big Book or the Twelve Step Book and contacted no one to sponsor me. AA calls it being a dry drunk.

"I lasted for seven years until 1990 when I married Powell. He was convinced I wasn't a drunk because he never saw me take a drink. That's all an alcoholic needs, someone to tell them she doesn't have a problem. It's like getting a Get Out of Jail Free card in Monopoly."

Sara tugged on her ear. "This next tale is called reciting my First Step for beginners. I organized a party inviting all the neighbors to celebrate our mailman's retirement on August 5, 2003. By four o'clock another neighbor and I had tasted most of the wine to make sure it was good enough. We had a dozen bottles each of white and red available. I was drunk before the first guest arrived. The mailmen stayed in the kitchen drinking more than their share. I'd move a bottle from the kitchen into the front room for the neighbors. Every time I went in there, someone would comment on the unusual reason for the party, a mailman's retirement. About the third time I heard it, after I put another empty wine bottle out on the back porch's empty cooler, it struck me. I was an alcoholic in need of help.

"I found a meeting the next night, kept going, bought all the books and looked around for a sponsor. I volunteered at an AA prison program where I met a sober woman who volunteered too. She'd been sober twenty-two years. I asked her to sponsor me and she agreed. I haven't sponsored anyone successfully but the program works for me. I practice the twelfth step by sharing at meetings. The AA Program isn't easy but it's simple enough to follow."

"Tell him how long you've been sober," Betty said.

"Fourteen years last August," Sara said. "But I haven't convinced these two to share in the rewards."

Rick voiced his concern. "Isn't it difficult to maintain your sobriety when they keep drinking?"

"It certainly is!" Sara said. "And Nancy is a spendaholic. Besides, Betty is always on one emotional binge or another. I pray for them."

"She always drags us along to meetings." Betty complained. "We're less shy when we drink. Our third husband would put a bottle of wine on the kitchen counter as a signal that he wanted sex that night. We can't go to a party without getting high first. Tonight was an exception. We arrived sober."

Nancy said, "When you're at a meeting, you just close your ears. Sara's right about the spending though. Your husband needs to do all the grocery shopping, otherwise you'd come out with a three-hundred-dollar pile of food for just one week with only two of you to feed. You think it's because you were so poor as a kid. Sara says to just get over it, but it's not easy. Bookstores are impossible too. Your husband says okay, two books, but by the time you leave your arms are full of books that just jumped out at you. You buy self-help books for Betty and the rest for Sara's eclectic range of interests."

"Sara's got us pegged," Betty said. "We need a heightened sense of drama around us, which we are accustomed to handling. Otherwise life is too boring. We don't like to think about the past mistakes we've made—especially with men."

Rick recited the Fourth Step, "Made a searching and fearless moral inventory of ourselves."

"What else is therapy for?" Betty asked.

"Is that working out?" Rick asked.

"Not really."

Nancy coughed. "You just don't have any resentments against anyone. You believe in forgiving and forgetting."

"How can we forget something that has already happened?" Betty argued. "It stays in our brain. We can't wipe it out."

Nancy started crying softly, "But you try."

Rick took their hands. "Will you do this for me? Go to

every meeting Sara attends and share in the table's subject of the day. Nancy you need to unplug your ears. Betty, it's a lot cheaper than therapy."

Sara laughed. "That was easier than I thought it would be."

Nancy said, "You wish you possessed both of your personality traits. Sara, you admire your steadiness and, Betty, you wish you had more courage to forage for answers. Rick, would you say you're the weakest of the three of you?'

"You may be the healthiest." Rick wanted to start the main session. The grandfather clock struck seven. "You're ready to acknowledge your gifts and recognize the power of other ways to face life's dilemmas.

Betty spoke rather loudly, "We don't think we're better or worse than you two. We are more independent. Maybe braver too?"

"Do you have the courage to change the things you can?" Rick asked.

"Do you think we can?" Betty laughed.

"Do you mean we should make a sustaining friendship in spite of all our differences?" Sara folded her hands tightly.

"Absolutely," Rick said. "That is exactly my goal. Have you seen 'The Man of LaMancha' musical?"

"Yes," all three answered in unison.

Rick nearly applauded. "His family and lawyer brought out a mirror for him to face reality. Shall I do the same for you three?"

"Are we ready for this?" Betty stood up as did her friends.

"We'll wait until all of you are ready," Rick said.

"Let's try something else first." Rick wandered over to the bookcases nearest the door and seemed to choose a book at random. "Would you all be willing to try the AA Big Book's Step Four?"

"Maybe," Nancy and Betty said together. Then Betty laughed heartily while Nancy blushed.

After moving the coffee table back in front of the couch, Rick laid three yellow legal pads on its surface. "As I read, why don't the three of you make notes?"

"Sounds easy enough," Sara was the first to reach for a pad. She took a pen from her purse.

'You can do that," Nancy said. "Maybe you'll just draw my answers."

"Whatever," Betty said. "Sara, do we have two more pencils in that suitcase we call a purse?"

Rick began to read the Fourth Step, "The index says, 'Step Four is an effort to discover our liabilities.' And strengths," Rick added. "Are any of you constitutionally incapable of being honest with yourselves?"

Betty spoke first, "We were surprised when we noticed we were lying to ourselves about Christmas miracles—of all things. Two miracles we claimed were acts of thievery. One time we were grocery shopping with a friend, who we later found out was being paid by Nancy's husband to spy on us. Anyway, we put Christmas trees in our trunk from the parking lot, meaning to pay for them with the rest of the groceries. Both of us forgot? We didn't bother to go back in and pay for the trees. Another time when we were living alone, trying to spend only the money we had available for groceries, we asked the clerk to set aside the Cold Duck and cigarettes. When we got home they were in the bag. We should have driven back and paid for them, but instead we told ourselves it was another Christmas miracle."

Rick asked, "Are you capable of grasping and developing a manner of living which demands rigorous honesty?"

Sara said, "I think we can all agree that's why we came here tonight."

Nancy wasn't convinced. "What if Betty has too many grave emotional or mental disorders?"

Rick laughed. "Have you been reading the Big Book?"

"Some," Nancy admitted.

"Us too," Betty echoed.

"We each want to run the whole show," Sara said. "Betty gets angry when she doesn't get her own way. Nancy wallows in self-pity, and I become indignant."

"Write that down, Sara," Rick said. "Do you admit to mostly a confused state of being rather than feeling in harmony with the world?"

"Selfishness and self-centerness make all of us fail." Sara re-buttoned her suit jacket.

"And retaliate." Betty tugged the hem of her skirt down.

"And just get hurt." Nancy sniffed. "You never forgave Mother for taking your full length mirror. After you eloped with Johnny, you were excommunicated from the church. Your brother-in-law, Etta's husband, sat next to you on the first Sunday after you eloped. The priest preached a sermon about you specifically. He said your lapse in judgment was due to reading books not on the approved Catholic list. Years earlier, he was the priest you had reported to his superior. You worked for a pediatrician one summer and this same bloke came in to pay the bill for a single mother, and—his child? You no longer wanted to receive communion from his hands. In fact, you thought he should be unfrocked. So you went to confession with the parish pastor, who said you were committing the sin of scruples. After the sermon the day after your marriage, Don Schultz wouldn't speak to you as you left the church. You went back home to pack up your clothing. Mother had taken everything out of your room she wanted. You had talked a shoe store out of the full-length mirror. Remember, you told him about drawing a picture of yourself with just Mother's quilt draped around you? That was the mirror you stood in front of. Mother said the Bishop told her not to give you any wedding presents, either.

"Even Johnny said you would need to forgive them. You didn't see why. But you were miserable and homesick. He told you to ask the Lord to be your Savior if you wanted help. So you did in a perfunctory manner. Nevertheless, your soul experienced an immediate flood of peace. Tranquility seemed to fill the entire world. You are thankful to Johnny for leading you to the Lord. He later denounced his faith—after your divorce."

Rick moved the tissue box closer to Nancy's side of the coffee table. Then he got up to tend to the stove. "I always need to turn up the thermostat at night."

"I don't live up to my highest aspirations," Sara said.

"Who does?" Betty was still able to laugh.

Rick rejected the pillows; instead, he sat next to them again at the end of the couch. "With a Higher Power as our Director, we all might feel a somewhat deflated ego, which leads to wonder what we can contribute to life. I promise you will find peace of mind if you ask for the Lord's will to be done every day."

Betty lowered her head. "Don't you think we want to

be rid of things in ourselves which block our progress?"

"Okay," Rick prompted, "Write down all the damaged or unusable parts of your personalities."

"For instance?" Sara asked pen in hand.

"Flaws," Rick said. "Do you admit to any, such as resentments and fears, which make you spiritually sick? List people, institutions, situations, and principles with which you were angry. How did your self-esteem, pocketbooks, ambition, including personal relationships suffer? Make three columns, one for resentments, one for the cause, and one for how it affected you—such as your security, fears, or self-esteem. Go to it."

Nancy and her friends got busy. Sara wrote her list first and was about to hand it to Betty.

"No, no," Rick said. "Each of you use a separate tablet." As they continued their task, Rick stated some of the insights he'd gained from the Big Book. "We squander the hours we could have made worthwhile. When harboring negative feelings we shut ourselves off from the sunlight of Spirit. We have to become anger free, or it is fatal to our well-being. Resentments are like swallowing poison and hoping the other person dies. Ask your Higher Power to help you show others the same tolerance, pity, and patience you would grant a sick friend. Now take a look at your own mistakes in each angry episode. Were you selfish, dishonest, self-seeking, or frightened? Where were you at fault? We need to avoid hysterical thinking or giving advice. If we continue to harm others, we cannot begin a new life. Are you willing to straighten things out with those you have injured? Now add a column or start a new sheet with columns for your personality traits, negative and positive."

When each of them had placed their finished Four Step inventories on the coffee table, Rick continued.

"Remember you have decided to go to any lengths to find a spiritual path to a better way of living, a new freedom and a new happiness. If you have a sincere desire to set right the wrongs you will be able to demonstrate your good will. God is doing for us what we could not do for ourselves."

CHAPTER FIFTEEN
SARA POWELL

SARA CROSSED HER ARMS. "Abraham Lincoln said, 'Character is like a tree and reputation like its shadow. The shadow is what we think of it; the tree is the real thing.'"

Rick asked her to read her Fourth Step out loud.

"I'd rather not, right now," Sara said. How could she tell her friends of their intrusion on her life and time for writing? They constantly hounded her with plans and luncheons, excuses to go to museums over and over, and to everyone else's book signings. They both made her life a little more difficult. She wanted to shout sometimes for them to leave her the hell alone. She could allow them when she was finished with her goals for the day, couldn't she?

"Let you read yours," Nancy said. "Under 'resentments' you wrote: Mother, Daddy, your first husband, your oldest son, and the ex-wife of your second son. In the 'cause' column you listed Mother, for ignoring you, Daddy for never hugging you, for your oldest son estrangement and for the wife of your second son you listed hatefulness and jealousy. You haven't told him why you think Carl just stopped contacting you. He lives near Tucson now.

About seven years ago he and his wife were in Lansing for Christmas. They hadn't told you they'd be near. On Christmas Eve, the favorite nephew of his wife Pat died of an overdose. He'd been dead an hour or two before Carl tried to revive him. You guess trauma like that just changes a person's life. You sometimes wonder if Carl wasn't inordinately fond of the nephew too. That would have just exaggerated the injury to his soul."

"You handled the loss of your son quite well. What were the results of your list?" Rick was taking notes.

Nancy continued as if sharing a book report, "Mother's inattention never gave you a basis for loving others, Daddy's not touching you didn't add to your self-esteem, Carl's elimination of a loving interaction further eroded your self-image. Of course, Tom's ex-wife and her constant contention made it difficult to visit your son and his children." Nancy pouted. "You were honest."

"I believe you," Rick said. "You have two other columns, right?"

Nancy nodded and flipped over the first page of her tablet. "For negatives you put: lack of courage to stand up to people, illogical thinking, and letting your impulses rule the day. Under positives you wrote: pleasing, entertaining, an artist's temperament."

"Did you notice?" Sara found herself forced to say, "Nancy listed the negatives first?"

Rick nodded. "Who wants to go next?"

Betty snatched her notes off the table. "We wrote this as a private memoir, but we understand the ameliorative effects of confessions. We hope all of you are able to stand the brutal truth. Under resentments, Tanya, Sara, Nancy, all Nancy's husbands in a group, all our un-constant lovers as a group, Nancy's first son, her daughters-in-law, unsuccessful therapists as a group, Republican's greed, voter's apathy, lying and cheating as a group." Betty let her ornery laugh ring out. "So, causes as listed across from each interference in our life: paltry attention, false friendship, lack of appreciation, lack of integrity, dishonoring his mother, unrequited hatred, lack of funds, the worst sin, maybe the next, unforgiveable." Betty lifted her head, chin jutting a bit before reading the results: "frustration, anger, disgust, hardening of our heart, mistrustfulness of men, grieving, an unforgiven part of our soul, distain, concern for our country, the waste of time and energy listening to the perpetrators."

"Honestly done." Rick smiled before saying, "And your second list?"

"Sara, we listed the negatives first too. Could that mean we're practicing humility? We're impatient, egotistic, prideful, not easily bullied, righteous, willing to ask for forgiveness from a Higher Power who will need to forgive Nancy's daughters-in-law until I'm able to forget their injuries, penny-pinching, more generous with available funds, militant in our anger and lacking the ability to trust motives."

Sara punched Rick's shoulder. "Her list sounds like a job-interview, listing her worst qualities in a positive light."

"I'm afraid so, Betty." Rick reached for her notes. "I couldn't keep up with your rapid recitation." Then he turned to Sara. "Your turn, are you ready?"

"I guess," Sara said. "My resentment lists first, outside activities; second, demanding friends; third, lack of time to write; fourth, agents' rejection of my novels; fifth, publishers ignoring my efforts; and sixth, my family's complications needing my attention." She sighed. "I repeated one cause for all of them, 'writing career.'"

"And the results," Betty grumbled.

Nancy was biting her fingernail.

Sara shrugged her shoulders. "Never being good enough to be picked up by a traditional publisher with distribution chains. The knowledge that I am not a completely functioning person."

Rick said in an upbeat tone, "I have another ploy before we face the mirror and reality. Who is willing to try?"

All three women shook their heads.

"It will work like magic," Rick said.

Nancy said, "You just like magic."

"No pain involved, right?" Betty's voice echoed her suspicions.

"You will laugh, I promise." Rick opened a concealed door next to the exit. He brought out a long black cape. "It's almost as big as a tent," he said. "Now join your hands, standing in in a circle around me. I'll drape the cape over your heads and shoulders."

Rick noticed his hands were shaking as he held the cape above their heads. He let it down slowly.

"Too dark," Sara said.

"Stay just a minute," Rick encouraged.

"They've let go of my hands." Sara struggled with the cape, trying to dislodge the cover.

Rick held her close for a minute. "You are sufficient in yourself," he said before sweeping the cape away from them.

Sara sank to the floor. Nancy tried to rise but Betty took over. "How dare you! We know your game. Is Tanya your pimp? You're trying to end our friendship by seducing Sara."

"Is he?" Nancy asked. "That's just not nice."

Sara was breathing heavily. "At least I'm not bored any more. Maybe if we'd gone out to dinner or horseback riding. Instead, we have all this drama contained in one room. Where's the action?"

Rick laughed. "At least we have character arcs."

Sara shook her head. "No. All we're doing is reciting back story. But, Rick has done us no harm."

"Yet!" Betty stomped around the room. "For all we know he's ready to poison two of us."

"You don't think so," Nancy said. She took Rick's hand. "Does he mean to harm you?"

"Not in the least," he said. "I know how to bring all three of you closer than you've ever been."

Sara was standing near the hall door as if ready to leave. Nancy put on the red cape. Betty was already in her boots. Sara wrapped her scarf tightly around her neck before pulling on her gloves. Wait," she said. "Before I give up on this visit and all the shenanigans, let's try his mirror."

Rick broke down. "Sorry, sorry. I'm not supposed to get so emotionally involved."

Betty stroked his back. "We're sorry we offended you. Get your mirror out. We're ready for more reality. Improvements are after all welcomed, aren't they? Did you notice our lack of confidence motivates us to check everything out by asking innumerable questions? When we make a mistake, we even ask, 'Okay what have we learned?' and 'Don't make that mistake again.' We are our own worst enemy."

Nancy bent down to give Rick her handkerchief. "Sara has always been the catalyst. Let's do it."

The three women herded together as Rick turned a wall panel around to face them. A floor to ceiling mirror filled the back side.

They stood silently for several minutes.

Rick broke into their contemplations. "What do you see?"

"You are just one," Nancy said.

"How long has Sara sanctioned our multiple personalities?" Betty knew every psychological term in the book from her countless therapy sessions. "Will being one create less misunderstandings and conflicts? This oneness thing might be doable."

Rick said, "I thought I could help you form a cohesion satisfactory to all of you. You've been suffering a multiple emotional disorder caused by an extreme sense of loneliness."

CHAPTER EIGHTEEN
SARA POWELL

"WHY DID IT TAKE SOMEONE like you to pull us together?" I rubbed my face to erase the last traces of their visages from the mirror's reflection. "Now how will they manage?"

"I'll help you set boundaries. You will be the *only* one to hear their input," Rick said. "Nancy will paint. Betty might take over your love life. She'll settle down by accepting your lowered, age-appropriate sex drive. She won't need to visit therapists anymore because of your steady hand and deep faith."

"Peace will reign." I could smile. "They're both happy. I never imagined they would abandon me. So if we share one soul, why did they still drink and not acknowledge the Lord's presence?"

"Don't you feel in sync with their souls?"

"I'm all three? Is that why you listened all afternoon, to build trust?"

"I found only you were aware of the different facets of your inner characters. Nancy demanded to paint without being burdened with other chores. Betty couldn't maintain your level of integrity in relationships. You understand your own failings while showing the most compassion for both of them. I trusted you."

I could feel my grin again. "I suppose Powell might find me less interesting as an assimilated person. Thank you, though."

"And our Higher Power," Rick said. "Come and sit down. I still have a few questions."

"I did think once when Betty had embarrassed me in front of a church member that I could write my friends' memoirs to help them see who they were."

"Journaling does help dispel Multiple Personality Disorders for many people." Rick took my hand, leading me to the couch.

"Are you writing a book about me?"

"Maybe for a psychological journal. Do I have your permission?"

"Will you change our names?"

"Oh I already have. Did you notice Nancy's, Betty's, and your last names all start with a 'P': Peach, Pozner, and Powell"?

"Probably so we wouldn't be confused when we used monogramed towels." I laughed for the first time in the Pleasure Dome. "Or when we laid our heads down to sleep on the embroidered pillows. I sound like I have three heads. One of the positive sides of MPD is that sharing our thoughts with each other will stop the ruminating energy drain."

Rick agreed. "You certainly triggered different thinking processes in each of your personalities. The changes in your voice and face clued me into who was in control, but the use of different pronouns made it a lot easier to deal with." Rick still held my hand. "Dissociative Identity

Disorders can be long lasting. Personality disorders are characterized by rigid patterns of thought and behavior. Because of their inflexibility and pervasive patterns, they can cause serious problems and impairment of function for the persons who are afflicted with the disorder."

I blushed and hung my head. "Nancy can paint. Betty feels raw passion. All I can do is write."

Rick said. "Writing is not a stupid occupation. You observe, speculate, invent, create, and summarize the world for others."

"When did I allow Nancy and Betty to begin?"

"Remember telling me about Sally, when you were young? I wish you had kept a journal. We might have been able to pinpoint the day."

I shed my gloves and neck scarf. "I don't keep a journal, but as a writer surely most of who I am is written down. Some accounts are even published."

"Do you have a tape recorder?" Rick asked. "I wish I had gotten your permission so we could have played back this session. I'm sure you would have heard the shift in voices."

"Where did I go, when one of them took over?"

"I've read some patients, sorry clients, recognize time lapses. However, I think all three of you are aware of each other at the same time. Is that true?"

"I did feel embarrassed by both of them at times." I kicked off my boots. When I stood, Rick helped me take off my cape. "You're no doubt right. Was there ever a possibility that you would have chosen one of them to take control?"

Rick took my hand in his again. "You were always the most encouraging and accepting of them. There was never a doubt that you would overwhelm Betty and Nancy with your good sense."

"Why should I keep a journal now?" I tied up my hair again with the red barrette. "Is there a danger of them returning to the forefront?"

Rick shrugged. "Journaling isn't for everyone, but you might discover a way for both Betty and Nancy to voice their complaints about decisions which might affect them. Make sure you keep the content private."

"Or people will know I'm crazy?"

"It is important to your well-being to get disturbing thoughts and feelings out of your mind so you can see them. There is never a requirement to share what you've written for your private edification."

"Like taking out the garbage." I unbuttoned my suit jacket. "Not that you would want your neighbors to go through the trash bags."

"Exactly," Rick said. "You might get a different perspective on problems when you see them written down. Writing certainly releases the tensions ruminating thoughts create. There is a wide array of therapeutic approaches that often include individual and group therapy, family involvement, experimental activities using art or music, body image therapy, even spiritual integration."

"Why do I have this disorder? Why doesn't everyone when faced with overwhelming events in their lives?"

Rick's hands were in his curls again. "Your ego could be considerably more fragile than other people's. Does it take a long time to recover from what feels like a brutal attack?"

I laughed. "Ten years, if you measure the time between marriages."

Rick crossed his arms. "Do you feel you experienced an intensely hard time controlling anger?"

I reached for one of the half-filled writing tablets on the coffee table. "I better write this down for you. I'm not going to remember them in the right sequence. You know I've been married for going on twenty-eight years to Powell. His first name is the same as my first husband's, the father of Nancy's—my boys. One time when I was shouting at him about something I yelled, 'John, John Peach,' instead of Powell. At the City Club, I introduced him to a writing partner who is an opera singer. I was pretty nervous so I said, 'Jeannette, this is John Peach.' Powell said, 'No, it's not.'"

"We carpeted after I gave up drinking because the light blue rug had too many spots of red wine from all the Mathematics and Physics Department's parties. The new carpet is red, which by the way is the color of my kitchen. I don't think writers should spend their time cooking. I do hate to cook. My food tastes like the pan—pretty bad. I had the kitchen painted barn red as a stop sign to not go in there. When the painter opened the paint can, he said, 'This can't be right.'"

"Back to the re-carpeting disaster—it's exactly like moving. You have to pack up all your belongings so they can rip out the old rugs and nail down the new. Powell didn't want the hassle. He likes his peace and quiet to conjure up mathematical-physics theories. He wasn't sealing the bottom of the boxes right or fast enough. At one point I gave up and threw the scissors at him, narrowly missing the man I love most in the world.

"Another time, on our first anniversary, March 23rd, Powell invited his daughter over. The 23rd is his birthday, too. I threw an entire set of dishes into the kitchen, scarring up the cabinets bad enough to need replacing. He picked up all the broken pieces. The man is a saint, even if he is Jewish. The next time I was angry enough to throw dishes, he wasn't home. I thought, well I'll take them down into the basement and break them in the utility tub. It seemed like such a lot of work, I gave it up before I started. So, I went shopping for clothes, until I had bought out my anger. Horrible, I know.

"When the boys were teenagers in Jackson, I arranged for them to go to the community college for extra credit during the summer months—mainly because one of their math teachers asked to take Nancy to lunch. The subject was her brilliant boys, both of whom he thought would end up in jail if she didn't do something. They had not gotten into any kind of trouble. Maybe their intelligence produced some amount of fear in their less endowed teachers. The fact she was a single (divorced) mother was mentioned too. Usually the boys rode the bus to and from home to college. I can't remember why, maybe I was attending a class at the college during the winter, but I drove them both home during a snow storm.

"It was not unusual, they were fighting. Somehow it got out of hand and Carl, the oldest, started shouting at me! I panicked. I was frightened. My parents never yelled. They just shut up when they were angry. Silence can be terrifying too. Anyway, I stopped the car and told Carl to get out. Perhaps Betty had been drinking. I certainly wasn't thinking kindly. He was given a ride home by strangers, but he was thoroughly chilled. I know he remembers the cruelty to this day.

"Another time when they were even younger in South Elgin, Tom told me Carl had hit him. I went into their bedroom and told Carl, 'Next time pick on someone your own size!' He punched me right in the jaw. We both sat down and looked at each other, knowing we were both in the wrong.

"Years later in the first condo I planned to buy, I was upstairs rushing to dress for work. The boys were making their own breakfasts getting ready for school. Then our dumb cocker spaniel yelped as if he were kicked. Betty yelled down to ask what had happened, stormed into the kitchen and either didn't ask for an explanation or didn't believe the story Carl told. He had repeatedly said he wanted to go live with his dad. Betty said, 'Call him.' Later the youngest, Tom, told me the dog was under Carl's foot when he stepped backwards. It had been an accident. I should have known. Nevertheless, Berry's unreasonableness resulted in Carl living with his dad for nearly two years. Finally, after his dad remarried and Carl wasn't getting enough care or attention, he called me to come home.

"It was tough. They would call me at work saying they were going to run away from home, one at a time after they'd been fighting. Betty called her therapist at the time. He told her to go home and ask the boys what they wanted for supper. Sure enough, no threats were carried out. Carl was terribly unhappy. They both were. I sat down with Carl and we made a list of what was wrong and what we could fix. Tom comes out looking like the brighter of the two, but I don't know. Carl's style of facing life was just different than Tom's. Tom saved himself from pain with a sense of humor which Carl didn't possess. Carl did teach himself chemistry. His high-school teacher called to complain he was too far ahead of the class, I had no idea. I suggested they advance him to the next level, which they did of course.

"When Betty married for the third time, I hoped her

new in-laws would contribute to the boys' college education. They had two homes, one up north and one near Detroit. Of course they were living on their retirement incomes from teaching and couldn't help if they had wanted to. The problem was when the boys applied for student loans, the combined income of Betty's husband and herself disqualified them.

"Somehow, Carl did attend Michigan Tech in the Upper Peninsula. Tom insisted he would drop out of high school, if I didn't do something. Tom was given an IQ test and the SATs. The scores placed him in the upper two percent of the nation. He was sixteen. I met with two admissions professors, one in Lansing and another in Ypsilanti. Someone told me to go directly to the President's office at Eastern Michigan. I talked to his secretary and Tom was admitted.

"The high school in Jackson called Tom and Betty in to argue about the importance of a high-school diploma. One of the statements was that Tom would miss keeping in touch with his friends in Jackson—something he would rue the rest of his life. I thought Tom was better off not knowing them and would find friends at college and later in the widened world I hoped he would inhabit.

"After Betty divorced her third husband, Carl left college to enlist in the Navy. I had to sign for him, because he wasn't yet eighteen. I thought Carl would benefit from the structured environment. He missed a strong father figure. I raised my boys to find their own moral compass, but Carl floundered. I knew Tom would be killed by his superiors if he had joined any gun-toting military unit.

"Let me give you an example of Tom's inherent stubbornness. He was about two and would put his fist in a planter on the coffee table, no matter how Nancy confronted him. John took over, but Tom looked him right in the eye and stuck his hand in the dirt. John used his big hand to blacken Tom from his waist to the back of his knees. Nancy decided never to involve their father in any discipline from then on.

"John was not an evil man. He had been abused by his mother. She bore seven children to her inventor husband, who lived in Kansas City, while she managed a farm she loved. John built and lit a rubbish fire too high which frightened her, I guess. She held matches under each of his fingers until they blistered."

I broke down. "The frustrated cruelty caused immeasurable harm in our families."

Tanya entered the room but Rick waved her away.

He said, "We often relive painful emotions when we recite the past. All those mistakes are history. Your insight into the motivations of your family helped you to forgive their shortcomings. You have a bright future ahead of you now. Your multiple personalities added to your inability to control your temper, because all three were riled. Now you only answer to one."

"I'll be seventy-eight in May." I hiccupped trying to regain some control.

Rick laughed. "Nevertheless, you cannot add or subtract a minute of your life. Name three things you enjoy about your life now."

I wiped my cheeks with a napkin left from supper. "Powell, Tom's love, and knowing my granddaughter, Katrina, and grandson, Nikolai."

Rick stood and went to the door. "Tanya," he called into the corridor.

"Are you all right?" Tanya asked me when she arrived.

"I am," I said. "But, I don't think I'm ready to face the world right now."

CHAPTER NINETEEN
RICK FITZGERALD

RICK ASKED TANYA to bring in bedding for me. "This couch pulls out into a good bed. Could you stay with us until morning?"

"I didn't bring a change of clothes," I said.

"Never mind that," Tanya motioned for Rick to leave. "I'll bring you a nightgown and robe."

Later Tanya climbed into bed next to Rick. "Have you saved them?"

Rick rolled over, draping one arm over her waist. "Time will tell. I hope I did the right thing by placing Nancy and Betty in Sara's hands, so to speak."

* * *

SARA POWELL

I fell into a deep slumber as soon as I was prone. My dreams allowed Betty and Nancy a platform for venting.

Nancy was wiping her face of tears. "You don't like these emotional traumas."

Betty pushed Nancy aside. "We've achieved a major breakthrough, you idiot."

"You can say this now." Nancy knocked Betty's shoulder. "Stop disrespecting you. You are the troubled one. What is it you want?"

"Silence," Betty laughed. "Like a good servant, just be there. Sara will let you paint. Rick was worth every penny she spent on him, if you'll keep quiet. We were worried he was wasting her time. Time is such a relative term. As we get older, it seems to speed up. A day feels like a minute, a month not even a week, and a year—maybe a month in June."

"Maybe you felt a loss of time when Nancy or I were in control." I hugged my pillow.

"Did you know you were one when Tanya asked you to meet her husband?" Nancy asked.

"What does it matter?" Betty threw my pillow to the floor. "We're worried about not being able to satisfy our sexual cravings."

"They're not as rampant as when you were younger," I admitted.

"Speak for yourself," Betty retorted. "Our head still believes we're eighteen."

"You didn't have sex until you married at twenty," Nancy reminded her."

"Both of you stop your yammering." I leaned over the side of the couch to retrieve my pillow. "I need to rest in peace."

"What are you supposed to do while you're sleeping?" Nancy asked.

I waved my arm at them trying to stop the intrusive chatter. "Magically disappear."

"Oh no," Betty said. "We haven't had a chance to comment on this new arrangement."

Nancy rolled over, pulling the covers over her head, saying. "You get to paint. That's all you care about."

Betty got up and stomped around the room, throwing my pillow at the closed drapes. Then she went to the bar, filled a glass with brandy, drank it and threw the glass at the mirror behind the bar. "We're still here, Bitch."

I stood beside her, claiming priority in my mirrored image. "And who do you see now?"

"You," Betty said. "But you haven't answered our question. What do we do about sex?"

"I'm married to a good man," I said. "Wait until he initiates sex."

"Won't do for us," Betty said. "You better chain us to the bed, if you're willing to wait that long."

Nancy stamped her foot. "Stop that. You've always been too selfish and demanding. You think you know why you need each other."

I crawled back to bed. "Can you tell us in three words?"

Nancy giggled. "No, no, no. Do you remember when you lived in Huntley, Illinois? You were memorizing the Sunday missal. You went out and sat on the fence by the horses."

"Was that at the White Fence farm?" Betty asked.

"That's where Mrs. McClintoch taught me how to spell my name for the first time," I said. "I don't remember the man's name, but he was always around for me to talk to. He even had me stay overnight at his house in town. And he gave me a cloth pin of a little Mexican boy and girl."

"We had that pin for years," Betty said. "Whatever happened to it?"

I sighed. "He wanted to adopt us, but his wife wouldn't have it. I wonder if Mother would have allowed it. Maybe he saw how abandoned I was."

Betty scoffed. "What did we expect? The third daughter with a much longed-for younger brother. We were lucky they let us eat at the table."

"Maybe that's when you began to talk to each other," Nancy said.

Betty spoke loudly. "We know with Etta the beauty in the family and Jean the perfect housewife, the only personality we could be was a writer, artist, or whore."

I covered my head with the pillow. "So I became all three."

* * *

In the morning after I showered and had eaten breakfast with them, Rick invited me back into the Pleasure Dome room. "Did you dream any answers to your new life as a single entity?"

I got comfortable on the re-made couch before answering. "Nancy might be suffering from an empty nest syndrome by using oil painting as a hobby. Betty definitely would rather isolate than interact with people. Did I tell you why John and the boys were abandoned, the first John?"

"Do you need to tell me?" Rick asked.

"I think so. I told you he traveled, but I didn't tell you I handled everything. Tom almost died when the hospital gave him an infection when they took out his tonsils. Then Carl let go of a wagon handle while he was giving Tom his first outing. I had to rush him to the hospital to get stitches in his forehead. Another time I was washing windows and one fell out of the sash and cut my arm. It didn't bleed at first but I couldn't drive to the hospital. I had to plead with a neighbor to take me and watch the children. I remember she told me she had walking pneumonia.

"I read all the time. Once when Johnny came home, he picked Nancy up book and all and carried her into the basement to watch him work on his oscilloscope."

"What's an oscilloscope?" Rick asked.

"An electronic meter for measuring electric impulses, I think." I squirmed. "He got the flu one time, vomiting and bad diarrhea. He wouldn't bathe, but pulled Nancy down to the bed for sex. The odor was revolting. Betty decided then and there as soon as he left on his next trip, she would take the boys to a neighbor who was a certified welfare mother. She hoped never to see Johnny again in her lifetime.

"Betty's husbands and lovers always smelled bad before she left them. She still remembers the smell of two of her lovers, the Italian and of course the bookman."

"That's your excuse for abandoning your children?"

"At the time, I thought John wouldn't want them. Nancy planned to get a job, buy bunk beds and return for them. She never thought John would ransom them for her return. As a bi-sexual, his interest was fleeting at best. His plan worked for a while, but Betty outsmarted him by staying married to Ken until John left."

"So how are you going to progress in life, now?"

"I think I'll be okay. At the university I went on a one-day retreat with all the other administrators. About twenty women sat around a squared-off group of tables to take an achievement test. There was only one bathroom. So I planned to finish first to be able to use the facility before anyone else. I rushed through the test, which resulted in my being labeled 'the most aggressive administrator in all of LS&A.'"

"Quite an achievement."

"I don't know. My forcefulness made me less useful at times. The Women's' Abuse Center in Jackson asked Betty to stop volunteering."

"Why?" Rick backed up from her on the couch.

"Betty took one woman and her two kids into her upstairs apartment in Jackson when both boys were teenagers. That was before wife-beating was declared a crime against the state. The woman's husband was allowed to stay in the house, so she had to leave. Betty told her to go home and when her husband finally slept to tie him to the bed and beat him around the head and genitals with her heaviest frying pan."

"Do you understand why they asked Betty to leave?"

"I do," I said. "They wanted women to come up with their own solutions so they would continue to take care of themselves. I don't see the need to be beaten into good sense. That was before the Marshall woman poured gasoline on her husband. Remember that?"

"Yes." Rick shook his head. "Were you ever a victim to violence?"

"Once," I said. "Betty was dating a married guy she worked with after her third husband. He had never acted weird, but one night he showed up high on drugs. He threw Betty around the apartment liked a wet kitten. She locked herself in the bathroom and told him to go upstairs, she'd be right up. When she heard him go up the steps, she went into the kitchen and called 9-1-1. They told her to stay on the line and call him. After Betty told him she'd called the police and he left, Betty told the policewoman I was all right. She advised me to seek counseling but thought the police dispatcher implied she was stupid."

"Complicated situations usually need help to be overcome."

"I know. After Betty had moved to the Clark Lake,

Tom was home from college and asked her why she didn't attend her feminist meetings anymore. Betty couldn't come up with an answer. When she drove up Route 127 to the Jackson meeting, she nearly drove off the road when she realized why she'd been avoiding them. She didn't feel equal to men anymore.

"I know I'm not as strong as some men, but I do feel as equal as any man feels to another man."

"Do you see any other problems with aggressively attacking life's problems?"

"I recently applied at the First Presbyterian Church for a training program for Stephen Ministers program. They interviewed me and then turned me down."

"Why?"

"I'd explained how I had called Seattle to inform the police about Nancy's grandson living alone off-campus at fifteen years of age. I also repeated Betty's Abuse Center story, I didn't even cover the most-aggressive administrator test result. I understand. Stephen Ministers don't try to solve anyone's problems. They just listen. When the minister rejected me, I brought up the Good Samaritan story about binding the man's wounds and arranging for his housing. But her decision stood."

"Do you plan to look for volunteer work?"

"I did join a Local Mission group at my church. At one meeting, they went around the table explaining how rewarding their work for others was. I told them, 'I've only attended meetings so far. Could someone put me in, Coach?' On the way to our cars one of the women told me she was tired of asking volunteers to man the Hope Clinic's distribution of food the first Saturday of every month. I agreed to take over the telephone task and accompany the volunteers when they allow people who have appointments to pick out a few groceries. It is heart-rending work."

"You've gained enough self-knowledge for now." Rick stood, so I did too. He walked me to the door. "When you need to talk, you know where to find me."

I bowed my head as he helped me on with my coat. "I hope the Lord and you know how thankful I am for your attention and real help in providing a safe haven."

— **End of Narrative Story** —

ADDENDUM

THE BACKGROUND STORY

EACH PERSONALITY HAD SUFFICIENT reasons to forge a new way of life out of their experiences. Nancy's unloved childhood and bisexual first husband propelled Betty to test out all aspects of her new identity. My refuge in books sustained them until they were ready to humbly give up their quests for personhood, which had brought them unhappiness, and to finally trust their Higher Power as I do. In order to explain the abandonment of Nancy's four- and six-year-old boys I've included more of their distinct histories.

BETTY POZNER
MAY, 1969
ELGIN, ILLINOIS

Men and their balls were a mystery to Betty. Men suffered from an obsession with balls. Boring baseball forced her to drink horrid, warm beer. Football, another senseless bashing of heads over a misshapen ball, caused spectators to roar at the gladiators' efforts to maim themselves. Basketball at least showcased bodies nicely, but deteriorated into dancing couples or deliberate shoving matches, resulting in sulkiness and anger throughout the ruined game. Golf, another excuse to vacate the house, knocked tiny white balls across acres of grass without the challenge of kept trees. An elitist game. The homeless could claim the flagrant lawns for tenting grounds. But no. Men had to have their balls—tennis, soccer, and the rest of them. Instead of aiming their masculinity at each other, they could have spent all that wasted energy where it belonged—between the welcoming legs of their wives.

* * *

Elgin, Boarding House
May, 1969

Betty did panic on her birthday, May 27, 1969. She no longer felt she had found a safe haven. Contact with John was deadly. He would take her for rides and threaten her, claiming she'd done a terrible job of mothering the boys—Carl had trouble learning. Rather than defend herself or the fact that Nancy had been mother and father to the boys, Betty often lapsed into narcolepsy as soon as John started speaking. She had no time to think. The families were pressuring her to return to John. He was buying a house for them across the street from his sister's. His practiced dominance did not allow him to accept even her claim of unhappiness. Betty had difficulty maintaining a non-submissive attitude around him. Nancy's training had been completed in those nine years of marriage under his thumb.

One evening when she visited the boys, John refused to let her see them and asked for her car keys. Betty gave him the keys and called her sister Etta to come pick her up. Etta had never been to the town where the children were staying and there was quite a delay.

John used the time to list Nancy's sins in a quiet fury. Frightened, Betty called the police to take her to their headquarters for protection. She also asked the sergeant not to hang up until the police arrived. Her sister drove up precisely when the cops arrived and after some explanations, Etta took Betty back to her room in Elgin. Betty had been thoroughly frightened and lost her umbrella in the scuffle.

She tried to get a loan for a car but had no money or collateral. John's lawyer called and she agreed to sign divorce financial papers as long as they did not include a waiving of custody rights. She also asked for the 1962 Dodge Dart to be put in her name and returned. John had purchased a brand new Plymouth Road Runner.

Betty decided to flee again. She couldn't visit Nancy's children without John's six-foot-five inch frame threatening each breath, each word with the children. She was motivated to further rebellion instead of the constructive plans Nancy had made. Betty told no one where she was going. But she would return. Betty felt over-programmed, unable to even disagree with him consistently.

"What are you doing?" Her spindly landlady complained.

"I don't want to stay here anymore." Betty continued to carry her belongings out onto the porch for a final packing of the Dodge.

"You've only been here a month. Are you going back to Johnny?"

"Of course not. He's always there when I visit the boys. I need time to think. I told him not to get a divorce. I'll come back."

"Well, I think you're throwing away a good thing. He was over here one day looking for you. He seemed nice and very concerned about your behavior. Does he know where you're going?'

Betty felt vindicated in leaving. John was even spying on her rooming house. She didn't want him to know where she was. She needed privacy to think, to construct—something.

The landlady huffed off. Betty continued to stuff the car. She didn't feel like singing as she drove off. She felt deprived of any belonging place. The bookman's town seemed a welcome place to run. It was far enough away to be hidden.

A motel sufficed for the first night and the next morning she found a furnished apartment for $80.00 a month. It was next to an air-conditioned branch library which she found out later in the hot summer was closed for lack of funds.

She made a list of everything she wanted to do, where to find a job and how to manage the money she had. At the top of the list was a visit to Robert's bookshop.

* * *

JACKSON, MICHIGAN
THE BIBLIOPOLE
JUNE, 1969

"—and then my cousin said to me, 'I'll be back to watch *60 Minutes* with you.'" Betty laughed.

Robert played with his mustache. "He might as well have said, 'Pass the peanut butter.'"

"Exactly. Here I'd loved him in secret for an entire year. Both our families would be scandalized. We'd been to bed twice. I'm just beginning to relax and enjoy all of it—his godlike blond beauty, his sexual prowess, my body's satisfaction—and he tells me it's all over—but he'll be back to watch television. And did I tell you, he was making a thing of it? I wasn't the only first cousin he screwed."

"You were the second, first cousin?"

"Yeah! Or maybe the third. And I was starving. So I called around to see who would deliver food. I got the chicken from the married motel's owner. I was crazy by that time. He made a slight pass and I got undressed again, making love to him. He left. I hid the chicken. My cousin came in to talk and I was ready to—just talk. Actually I was too tired to talk. I listened and went home the next morning."

"Are you sure this is what you want to be doing?"

* * *

JULY, 1969
FURNISHED APARTMENT NEAR LIBRARY
JACKSON, MICHIGAN

No matter how Betty progressed in independence, or even how the half-consummated loving of Robert grew, she could neither reconcile the need for Nancy's boys—which she felt was part of her bones—nor alleviate her sorrow, which was like nails under a comfortable mattress. She couldn't breathe properly.

So Betty contacted John. He thought he could change and wanted to try. Nancy asked to come back and he drove to Jackson to help her move back with him. Nancy had been gone without her boys for two months.

* * *

July, 1969
Schaumburg, Illinois

Endless rows of brick condos without a tree in sight took the heart right out of Betty. The first few steps into the new place were distressing. To keep her composure, she hurried to the front room window where John had placed a pot of yellow daisies.

Sweets jumped up and knocked the pot to the floor. Looking down at the mess she'd made, the kitten searched the room for someone else to blame. Then she ran around claiming everything, even sticking her nose down John's discarded shoes.

Carl and Tom were a pleasure to behold. Betty tried not to smother them in over-compensating attention. But, when they entered any room, she quit speaking to watch their pretty heads, meet their eyes if they glanced her way. She readily opened her arms to embrace them at the least excuse.

John didn't have it easy. Betty was looking for the changes he'd promised. Besides, she'd changed into a heretic, proclaiming immediate dissension to anything he advocated. He'd expected her to be repentant not truculent.

Betty wrote a letter to her sister Jean, who had moved away to California, to explain the unsettled state of their lives. "Well, I'm back with him and Carl and Tom. I found I couldn't live without Nancy's boys. Things are not even close to ideal between us. For the present they are tolerable. John knows everything is up in the air. I have not made any decision except that I must be with Nancy's children. I'm looking for a job and we'll be moving into a house across the street from his sister's. It has trees. I guess I should say don't worry. But listen if you want to worry a little, go ahead. I'm absolutely certain it will help no one. God knows (if you care to believe in such a drunken bungler), Johnny has been trying. Hope lingers 'I've heard it in the dreariest land.' But that's about it. I weigh 125 and he is below 190. You can see food does not provide all the comforts one's soul requires. I'm trying to build my own life now, not trying to live his in my half-shadow way. I do believe it would be ideal if I could fall madly, happily back in love with him."

As soon as the boys left, Betty would settle in the corner of the kitchen to call Robert. After she obtained a secretarial job near the airport—without John's blessings, she called Robert from work every day.

Robert Koelz wrote to Betty via a post office box in Plato Center. She hid the letters under a rock in a cemetery next to where Johnny and Nancy started their marriage in an old school house near a railroad track with a garden neither of them weeded.

In July during their continuing arguments, when John was backed into an ideological corner, he would say he and the boys would disappear—a very successful weapon. Betty would turn to pleading he not leave, not take the children away. After consulting with a lawyer, Betty decided to take legal action. She could get an injunction to restrain Nancy's husband from taking the boys but needed a divorce pending in the courts.

* * *

August, 1969
St. Charles, Illinois

Betty took the boys to Marie's house. John was served divorce papers the next Monday. He showed up at their parents asking to see the boys. As Betty walked into the screened-in back porch with Carl and Tom, John furiously grabbed Nancy putting his hand in her mouth and the other on the back of her neck. He tried to choke her.

The boys began to scream.

Udale pulled on John's elbow to dislodge his hold. As they went back into the kitchen, Betty heard Udale say, "That's not the way to be."

More turmoil followed. Who is patient or realistic enough to understand during the emotional storm of divorce? No one can shut a door of legalized life to immediately open a new one. Quite a bit of trading must occur before the gate can be shut on beliefs, material goods, friendships, and unfortunately children.

* * *

SEPTEMBER, 1969
KANE COUNTY COURT HOUSE
GENEVA, ILLINOIS

The courthouse was built in a Red Cross symbol with the court rooms at the four ends of the cross. The center section was open with marble fenced balconies along the halls of three levels of the courtrooms. Benches were placed along the walls, giving a view of the comings and goings of lawyers, juries, defendants, and plaintiffs.

John's family and cronies sat facing her. The women's restroom was directly to the right of them. Betty had no one with her. Brittle with tension, it was difficult for her to walk in a dignified manner past them when she needed to use the facilities during the long waits. Once inside the restroom, she did relaxing exercises in order to proceed at all. What an ordeal. Surely married people should be allowed to duel as the merciful means of ending a marriage.

Even though they were in closed chambers, the court scenes were frightening, unbelievably gross affairs. Betty was first to state her case. She tried to explain all she could: That John had never loved her, had tried to buy her loyalty. She felt like a legalized prostitute, but she wanted her children. The judge's questions later in the month-long hearing showed he had promptly forgotten or chosen to disregard any reasons she put forth for leaving her children.

A neighbor of John's sister said Betty had propositioned him on the dance floor in front of John and his wife. Supposedly, Betty had said, "Let's blow this joint. I can really turn you on."

Betty never used such cant phraseology. The man and his wife were undergoing the healthy trauma of marriage counseling, something she wished John would have agreed to long before Nancy left the children. Betty had tried to encourage the man telling him he was a fine man, not to worry, everything would be all right. Later Betty found in 1972 when she was again living with Nancy's boys, that the neighbor had asked for a large loan from John—over $2,000 and never paid it back. Betty supposed the man felt entitled for payment for the crime of perjury.

Another nervous neighbor testified that one afternoon she was explaining the etymology of the word "fuck," while Nancy's boys were walking in and out of the room— how it was used in the early English of Chaucer. Betty had been facing the door and couldn't remember Carl and Tom in the room at the time. Betty was always aware of them. This particular neighbor worked for John for four years after the divorce.

The licensed foster parents, with whom Nancy left the boys on April 20, 1969 for one afternoon and dinner, testified she was not a good mother because she left the boys in their care. When John moved out of their Ann Arbor home he gave them a road-race set, train models, exercising equipment, metal shelving, cabinets, couch and chairs, workbenches, dining room table and chairs, bric-a-brac, and bulky wooden toy heirlooms.

John's brother-in-law claimed Betty and he had gone to a bar one evening (it had been three o'clock in the afternoon). Also that Nancy's oldest son Carl flinched when he reached to stir something with a wooden spoon. This particular man propositioned Betty repeatedly. When Betty's lawyer asked him if that was true, he replied, "I wanted to see how far she would go."

After Nancy had signed off on the sale of the original house, without benefit of divorce, John loaned his sister and brother-in-law $4,000. They never paid it back.

When the fifth witness, John's sister Betty, entered the chambers, Betty leaned over to her lawyer and whispered, "I didn't rape her either."

The sister claimed Betty drank a full bottle of gin while visiting Nancy's boys one Saturday. At the time Betty was not a heavy drinker but it was hot and she had brought fixings for gin-and-tonics to show them how Sara's bookman made them properly. Betty left the bottle when she went home. Of John's clan of two sisters and four brothers, these two were the irreligious alcoholic couple.

John did not testify.

The emotional storms from the court scenes were so vivid even Betty's surroundings seemed tainted. On the road to work Sara found a common tragedy and wrote to Robert,

"A white cat died.

It lay by the side of the road,

Hind feet clasped, forepaws were too.

I drove on and the world
Fell into its allotted place.
Next day cat was strewn, crow-eaten
Only half-white now.
I smelled the blood of the cat.
It clung to the tires of my car."

Betty was losing. Her lawyer agreed she should appeal to John. Over restaurant pancakes, Nancy pleaded for the boys from their father. John was unmoved. He admitted obtaining custody was the only way he could get Nancy back.

Off the record on the day of his decision, the judge started by asking John if Nancy had returned. Then he commented that it must be nice for John not to be told by a woman when to cut the grass, explaining further how tiresome it was to have to chauffeur his own wife and daughter all over town. John cheerfully agreed. The judge then said Nancy was the only wrong party in the case, and because a decision had to be made and he considered her unstable, John would be awarded custody. He also pointed to Nancy's lawyer and said that in his last case he had given the children to the mother. So this time he was reversing the trend.

Nancy asked if ten years had not meant something. The judge said no, they had not meant a thing. The judge, Charles G. Siedel, is dead and buried today and his hopefully impotent hide resides in hell. His daughter roamed Elgin streets in early morning hours waiting for her favorite bar to open. The police consider her absolutely mad but harmless. Their only hope was that she would keep her clothes on for an entire day.

* * *

October 10, 1969
St. Charles, Illinois

The divorce decree was an inhumane document, describing John as appearing in his proper person, Nancy just in her person. Custody was awarded to John, a fit and proper person, while Nancy was deemed unfit and improper.

When Betty drove down the main street of the county seat, she took Nancy's emotional pulse and found it didn't scream with pain. Numb, she had no realization of the torn-asunder days ahead. The empty place where the boys had been had not opened its blackened doors to the tear-gutted echoing dungeon of heart beyond. Nancy left a second umbrella: it would have been too excruciating to retrieve.

It was suppertime when Betty arrived at Marie and Udale's house. Nancy had told John she would bring the children to him the next day. Sanity and anguish would have swamped her if she allowed him to actually take the children from her. As Betty tried to eat, the boys came up to the table. She told them the judge had given them to their father. They didn't understand. Nancy put her hand on the top of Tom's head and her arm around Carl. Betty felt the gulf of emptiness before her.

The day after the boys were gone, Udale hugged Betty's shoulder and said he would not help with any appeal as he had promised. Marie wanted to go to Florida and they needed a new car.

Nancy and John had agreed to save on lawyers' fees by dividing the furniture themselves. Sara was given her high-school graduation desk, typewriter and an antique telephone chair. John kept the birthday presents he'd given

Nancy throughout the years—punishment Betty supposed was part of his Baptist generosity. She wasn't surprised by the added viciousness. After all, how can a man say he loves a woman and take her children from her? His hatred embarrassed Betty for ever marrying him. He returned Nancy's clothes tied in knots.

* * *

OCTOBER 1969
ROOMING HOUSE
JACKSON, MICHIGAN

"Pain has an element of blank; it cannot remember when it began. And of course it never hopes to be cured," Unknown Quote.

Betty had fled to Robert's comfort. Crystallized snow crunched under the wheels of the white Mustang. The headlights scanned black giants of snow-iced trees assembled for a silent greeting. The two-story shingled rooming house stood forlorn in the chill, trying to appear resolute. Robert had arranged room rental with the diminutive landlady. Betty was assigned a large room furnished in huge threatening pieces.

Hiring was rather restricted near the holidays of 1969, but she found a temporary job at a public utility's home office. Her boss was a typical genuflecting executive. Betty unwittingly brought him an unacceptable cup of coffee since neither eating nor drinking outside the canteen was allowed. In sub-zero weather, the door to the building's roof was left open. When Betty complained of the windchill factor on the stairwell leading to the copy machine, her boss nervously said someone might want it open. When she was offered a permanent position, she read their secretarial manual which required girdles. She feared they might confiscate her earmuffs as socially aggressive in some future conservative purge.

Betty rose to winter's light, often making breakfast of tomato juice iced on the windowsill and cheese crackers hidden in the closet. Darkness would be four hours deep before she would return from Robert's shop for sleep. She dwelt in Plato's cave. Swiftly fled the days of morning brightness of her freedom. Now the stark hours of grief's tyranny tread darkly.

Funds were running low, so Robert and Betty shared turkey pot pies for Christmas dinner. She gave him her camera and he gave her a pair of his woolen mittens. The hours with Robert were filled with verbal adventures. The boredom of a stifling marriage did not prepare her for even the temperate conversations of the bookstore.

"Are the cobwebs flying again?" Robert leaned back in his worn swivel chair. Then tipping forward, hands clasped, knees apart, he glared at her to answer.

"Do you know how many times I've been told I think too much, I talk too much, I read too much, that no one can understand my disjoined conversation? Do I seem muddled to you?"

"No."

"I don't mind your repeating words correctly without breaking into what I'm saying. I read more than I've heard words and I think I do make up a lot of words."

"Like volumptuous."

"Well they usually are lumpy. I have great legs. I wish I could grow a mustache to gesture the way you do. *Wouldn't you rather have a plump and wholesome wench like me?* The first part goes something like, *See that fashion beauty there, so slim of hip and sleek of hair—*. I don't know who wrote it."

"You do eat."

"That's from being a farmer and harvest meals. I'm hungry now."

"You just ate!"

"I know. I weigh 130. When Nancy left Johnny, she weighed 125."

Robert strutted around the shop making obvious gestures at his slim physique.

* * *

Ed and Sasha were frequent visitors and book traders at the Bibliopole.

Ed announced his arrival, "Gee it's good to see you two again."

"He's not behaving you know," Betty said.

Everybody but Sasha hugged everyone. Sasha kept her composure in the face of such obvious hooligans. "Ed's been drinking all day with Joe and the other law partners."

"Good, you look great." Betty touched Ed's brightened face.

"Sherry, Sasha?" Robert handed Ed a glass. He and Ed talked about books. Robert explained the leads for buyers as well as giving excuses for not paying Ed for the ones he had already sold.

Sasha, tense as usual, wasn't entirely fond of these people of Ed's. She was impatient to finally be rid of all of them socially. They were both studying to be German professors. She hoped they would obtain positions in another state. Sasha, whom Ed had met in Germany, was already well on her way toward a doctorate, but Ed had been dragging his feet.

Betty was left with the task of making conversation with Sasha. It was always best to nod one's head affirmatively when speaking to Sasha with just the proper amount of *yes's* and *of courses* interspersed. Any sign of disagreement would bring the entire discourse to an immediate halt.

Betty didn't suffer long because the door opened again for Robert and Alice Shaw. Robert insisted Robert Shaw was Bernard Shaw's illegitimate son. Alice Shaw, just twenty-one, thought he was more in the mold of Sherlock Holmes.

Both Roberts expounded on a dialect of the Himalayas, who knew the experts and who was best at the dialect's nuances.

Betty sought relief in Ed's direction. "Ed, are you going to keep your promise?"

"Of course—what promise?"

"To see Robert's Uncle Warren."

Robert stopped talking to Shaw.

"Robert?" she asked glad to be in control of the conversation, "Wasn't your uncle in the Himalayas?"

Shaw got interested. "Let's all go."

"No." The bookman crossed his arms for a more stubborn stance. "I'm not going."

Alice kept her eyes on the bookman. "I'll stay with Robert."

"Oh no you won't." Betty said. "I know he could pass for Mark Twain, but he's mine and I don't know how to share. If he is going to stay here, he will stay alone."

Sans Robert Koelz, they took two cars to seek out the recluse, Uncle Warren, mostly to keep Sasha quiet—since it was on their way home. The snow sparkled in the midnight moonlight and their wine helped to convince them it was a sane thing to visit an eighty year old man this late at night. Of course even though he came to the door, he wouldn't let them in. Betty and Ed hugged goodbye. Betty took the Shaws back to her car.

Shaw was in a miffed mood, because he couldn't show off his expertise in language. He told Betty she was talking nonsense when she said she would never marry again. "You have shit for brains."

Betty countered even less intelligently. "Well, you are a shithead."

That did it.

As they came to a stoplight in the middle of Jackson, Mr. Shaw jumped out of the car and slammed the door.

Betty apologized to Alice. "I thought he could take it if he dished it out."

"I'm glad somebody besides me finds him pompous," his young wife answered.

Betty returned to Robert who was delighted things went so badly. He used the episode as a new piece of entertainment for his friends.

* * *

December, 1969
Jackson, Michigan

With her paychecks from Consumers Power, Betty leased a one bedroom apartment in a solid-looking brick building. There were two apartments on each floor. Old-fashioned knotty-pine paneled the Pullman kitchen. It reminded Betty of her cousin's cabin. To retrieve her meager divorce allotment of furnishings from Marie's garage, she returned with Robert to Illinois.

* * *

Hoffman Estates, Illinois

The children were living with John in a ranch house across the street from his sister in Hoffman Estates. Nancy wanted to give Carl and Tom their Christmas presents while she and Robert were there. Nearly three months had passed since the divorce. Betty left Robert Koelz in a pizza parlor about four blocks from where the boys lived. She had called John a week in advance and again before she left the pizza parlor.

When she arrived, Nancy's children were not home so she walked across the street to their aunt's house. The boys were playing with their cousins. Betty told them to get their coats on and explained to their aunt she had expected to see John. She had Christmas presents for them in the car. Betty explained she was taking them out to lunch at the pizza house.

Their aunt refused to let the boys go.

Betty didn't believe her. The boys had their coats on and she held the door open for them. Tom walked out ahead of her. She told him to hurry.

"Come on, let's run," she said when she heard their aunt yelling. Carl's fifteen year old cousin tackled him on the lawn behind her.

Betty was at the car and her husband's sister was running at her. Betty got in the car. Tom was already looking through the presents. The woman outside was pounding on the windshield, yelling at her. Betty couldn't believe it was happening.

Of course Betty should have stayed in the car, but the rage outside was frightening. Carl was still not in the car, but she drove to the pizza joint and helped Tom take in their presents.

Trembling she tried to explain to Robert but couldn't relate the events clearly before John and his brother-in-law came in about five minutes later. John and Betty ended up pulling on each of Tom's arms. Nancy let go first, trying to explain to the little boy she loved him as she handed him Carl's Christmas presents too.

* * *

ALBION, MICHIGAN
JOE WILCOX'S HOUSE
NEW YEAR'S EVE, 1969

On New Year's Day that year, a friend of Robert's, Joe Wilcox, invited them to keep him and his cat company. Alyce Katz was made a mail-order minister, so they treated her with due respect. Robert described her as resembling a small black yak. When she entered a room, she would meow a polite greeting. Joe would wool her around, rolling her on the Oriental rug, telling her boisterously how much he missed her. Such undignified behavior unnerved the cat. She would slink away whenever Joe's attention could be diverted. Joe would panic, unable to find her. Distraught he would stomp up the front stairwell, down the vacated servants' stairs to the basement, where they could hear him cursing unlit flashlights.

That night Joe directed Robert to the master bedroom as he intended to find Alyce Katz before retiring to the guest room. However Robert insisted they bunk in the guest room. His advances were unusual. Although they regularly slept together nude, this time he insisted on mounting her.

Of course Joe opened the door thinking they were in the master bedroom. Apparently, Robert Koelz wanted a witness to nothing. Betty could understand his need to prove virility but she didn't relish the need for deception.

In the morning they swept Joe's book-filled mansion from basement to attic to rid the premises of evil forces such as the strange lurking shadows left from the last tenant of the Episcopal mansion, who probably drilled the basement hidden vantage point to view any occupant of the toilet in the first floor wash room.

One of the results of the sweeping in of 1970's New Year was that Joe married—after forty years of single life.

* * *

FEBRUARY, 1970
JACKSON, MICHIGAN

Just in the nick of financial time a small felt-cutting factory hired Betty as a secretary. The plant was located in the country with an acre in front and nearly four behind, bordered by a willow-lined creek. The dwarfish water tower was hidden by evergreens. Maples encircled several tables laid out with a snow feast that promised picnics.

Betty expected the workers to be Walden inspired. Instead, they resembled the remnant performers of a defunct circus. A fat lady, over two hundred pounds, clad daily in emerald green, spread the width of her desk. She initialed everything in sight.

A lazy blonde flitted around the invoice files. As a child she'd been burned by hot tar which fell from the roof her father was fixing. She was badly scarred on one side and wore long sleeves even in the hottest part of summer.

A prancing black-mustached straw boss needed black boots and a whip to be elected ringmaster.

The factory foreman was a burly, mashed-face lion tamer. There also was a broken-limbed ex-trapeze artist mimic. He had cerebral palsy, which weakened his left side; natural disuse caused the muscles to be unformed. His name was Ken and he propositioned Betty daily.

Betty saw herself as the tightrope walker constantly falling out of the accepted social grace of her fellow workers. They were shocked at her announcement that the factory workers should be paid more than themselves, because they worked harder.

* * *

Another oddity of Betty's was that her cat, Sweets, had cured her of killing any living thing. She once thought a huge black ant was harming Sweets and stepped on it, feeling very protective. Sweets laid his head down next to the ant and tried to push it with his paw. Betty had killed his playmate.

Betty's boss at Felters would call her into his office to catch reoccurring spider occupants, which she took outside. That spring the factory workers told her there was a skunk under the dye storage shed. She told them to leave it alone and it would go home. The next day they told her it was a raccoon mother with babies and one of the men had shot it. She roamed the factory floor asking for the culprit. When they discovered she'd called the game warden, who needed the carcass to prosecute, they admitted they had her searching for a left-handed screwdriver—it had all been a prank.

* * *

One woman would arrive in the office each Monday with a weekend report of rod-beating her dastardly children. The picture on her desk showed them in Scout uniforms, unsmiling ramrod straight. Once when the out-of-town hierarchy of the factory was assembled in the boss's office, the woman started murdering flies, uttering rude adjectives to describe their habits.

Betty couldn't stand it, so she informed the tyrant that the poor things were at least no worse than murdering creatures a thousand times bigger, who beat their children as a weekend hobby. Her boss flew out of his office at her. Betty calmly faced him.

He stammered, "Killing, killing flies is all right." He returned to his visiting gods.

* * *

DECEMBER 1971
FURNISHED UPSTAIRS APARTMENT
WORKED FOR COMMONWEALTH ASSOCIATES

In a visit to Robert, Betty was all legs. In a black sleeveless dress with a lace-edged white collar, Betty revealed enough cleavage as she bent over to talk to Robert. Her hair had grown past her shoulders. Robert was in blue again.

"Still wearing round heels?" Robert straightened his cravat.

"I am. Chalked up quite a handful of engineers. Freedom, I guess. Or the need to prove I'm sexually attractive, because John acknowledged his bisexual tendencies. Losing Nancy's boys didn't keep me very sane, you know. I'm sorry marriage to Ken interrupted our friendship. I'd hoped being married would help me regain custody of Nancy's children. I guess Ken was jealous, because 'Robert says' came out of my mouth too often."

Footsteps were heard on the stairs leading to the bookshop.

Robert held up his hand to listen. But Betty yelled, "Harvey?"

"Yes," Harvey intoned in a low base.

Robert growled. "You've got to stop that. What if he was a customer?"

Betty got up and went to the door. "Harvey, buy something."

Harvey hugged her as he entered. He took the seat of honor and handed Robert a sack with two bottles of sherry in it.

"Hurray! I thought we were going to die of thirst," Betty said. "Give me the glasses, Robert. I'll wash them this time."

"No need, all is ready."

"He's not in a good mood, Harvey. I've been regaling him with my sexual exploits."

Harvey's movements were deliberately slow. "Who's being exploited?"

"I guess anyone that has sex feels used." Betty decided.

"Unless they're loved," Robert added.

"What is love?" Harvey asked.

"And who is God?" Robert countered.

Betty asked, "Is love all we'll ever know of God?"

"More sherry," Robert yelled.

Betty added, "J.C. said, 'God is love.'"

Robert held his glass up to toast the nonsense. "Well, sex is good for half an hour, then what?"

"Find friends and brag," Betty said. "But my damn ego is either exhausted or empty. Love is a nonsense word anyway. When a person hears, 'I love you,' the receiving person thinks, 'Oh, hurray, a blank check of acceptance. I can be myself. Everything about me this person adores.' So they let go and become their charming, brutally honest selves. Meanwhile the person who said, 'I love you,' thinks, 'My God! I've created a monster. How do I turn this off?' The one who said, 'I love you," only meant, 'Boy, I feel good when you say or do that specific thing.' But of course the short-cut language, 'I love you,' doesn't convey anything except confusion and false license instead of a specific direction or even a slim clue."

"Think about it. Instead of saying I'm in love, show what you mean: go the extra mile, listen with intent, do the chores, walk the dog, feed the cat, bring flowers, send cards, write letters, cook if necessary. Do the deed."

Harvey waved at Robert. "She does talk."

"Have you heard her sing?" Robert turned quickly to Betty. "Don't"

"When I sang God Bless America during my Viet Nam conscientious-objectors counseling sessions, the young men all fled to Canada."

Pete, another crony of Robert's, entered. They'd been too engrossed to hear him trip up the stairs. He wore jeans and a plaid shirt and carried two buckets of paint in one hand and brushes in the other. "Drinking? It's two o'clock in the afternoon."

"What's all that?" Robert asked him.

"You said the shelves needed paint."

"It's Saturday. What about customers?"

"What customers?" Pete asked.

Betty politely offered, "Pete, can I pour you a glass?"

"No."

"Well leave the paint!" Robert directed.

Pete set the buckets down in the middle of the doorway, leaving in a huff.

Betty continued the conversation. "I could hate

Nancy's husband, if I gave it the time. But life is too full not to explore."

"Do you know how to love?" Robert asked. "Were you ever loved?"

"You'll have to father me," Betty said. "Udale was too busy feeding us."

"I'm not old enough to be your father. I've never been associated with anyone your age or disposition. By the way, did you divorce Ken?"

"No, poor boy. I left him this August. Nancy's children visited for a week and they treated me like a favorite aunt. It's not Ken's fault. I miss the boys and think I married him so the court would let me have Nancy's boys. I even stopped counseling draft-objectors, because her lawyer didn't want Nancy's friends to appear radical."

Two voices are heard on the steps.

Robert yelled, "Ed, Sasha!"

"What if they are customers?"

Sasha appeared first. Definitely shorter than her husband Ed, by a head, her short dark hair was unstylish as were her black stockings and sensible shoes.

Ed hugged everybody, drank sherry, remembered Sasha and poured her a glass. He turned back to Robert. "We were in town so I thought we could drop in."

"Nonsense," Sasha countered. "We came specifically to see you, Robert."

"I'm honored, Sasha. I haven't sold any of those books you gave me on consignment. But of course you know it takes time."

"We can't stay long," she said.

Ed ignored her, sitting next to Harvey he asked Betty, "How is Nancy's custody fight going?"

"The lawyers are getting rich. Nancy lost again."

Sasha shook her head.

"She hasn't given up," Robert said.

Betty said, "Nancy was not a great mother. But she may get her children back soon. The boys' housekeeper, Mrs. Mac, and I talk. She told me she is thinking of quitting if Nancy can come back. She thinks Johnny would let her."

Robert's voice rose, "He'll expect her to be more than a housekeeper."

"I know. I've not been around the boys for almost two years—and now that I've left Ken."

Sasha stood. "Ed, we've got to get back home."

"I know, I know." Ed took Betty's hand and she started to cry. "It will work out."

Robert waved everyone out of the bookstore. He knelt on the floor next to Betty.

Betty grinned through her tears. "Proposing?"

"That would be big of me."

"Bigamy, a pun! Where's Harvey? He loves puns."

* * *

JANUARY 29, 1972
SCHAUMBURG, ILLINOIS
THREE BEDROOM HOUSE

After reuniting with John and Nancy's children on Carl's birthday, Betty ran into trouble again. She couldn't remember the exact party, but everyone was drinking heavily again. Eventually, Betty was in bed with John, his knees were near her ears, his huge cock sweeping her cheek. As he put it in her mouth he said, "When I'm drunk I don't care where I put it."

"Frigid." Betty thought it was a cold-hearted condition, or maybe a chilled limb or two. But frigid was the numbing of all senses by shock to the whole being—every level. Betty enjoyed every touch, every word of attention, never expecting to become a sensory dead creature. Her entire body no longer responded to the act. John didn't notice the change.

When she heard the truth, Betty knew it. The Baptist absolved himself of blame (the alcohol did it). He also implied not only which orifice but which gender. He didn't care if he had anal, oral, or normal intercourse. Sex was all the same to John drunk or sober, and the other person involved was more of an embarrassment than a pleasure.

After Nancy's boys left for school and he was gone to work, Betty called Robert. She told him what John had said, and that she had experienced the act of sex without a nerve responding.

* * *

1989
Ypsilanti, Michigan

When Betty was forty-nine and Marie eighty, Betty realized how little she meant to her mother. Marie was within ten minutes of her house, and after not seeing her for two years Marie hadn't even called. The cruelest part was Marie told Betty about how close she had been to her apartment. Betty was angry for months before she could calm down enough to tell anyone. Knowing Marie practiced Catholic self-flagellation, Betty called her. Betty told Marie she'd forgotten why she was angry. Marie gave a response Betty could have written out ahead of time.

* * *

Sara Powell
April 20, 1969
Bibliopole, Jackson, Michigan

On my way through Jackson, I stopped at a rare book dealer's I'd visited once before. The Bibliopole was housed above a liquor store, but a sign explaining "Bibliopole" designated the access door.

The steps were steep and a banister high overhead let the sound of speech within the shop reach the climber. The hall bulletin board was papered in graffiti, political and social.

Entering, I immediately faced the owner and speaker, Robert Koelz. He had kinky gray curls, a bristling mustache, and intense blue eyes. His face was pale and he used his hands while he talked as I imagined a Frenchman might. His voice was deep but crisp.

He interrupted his discourse with a man less dapper than he and rose from his desk to greet me. Robert's figure was youthful and his stomach as flat as an athlete's. He wore an open-throated linen shirt with a matching blue sweater. His pants were well-fitted with a trim pleat, while his shoes appeared store-box new.

After a warm hello and offer of a glass of sherry Robert introduced me to his friend, "This is my oldest friend. Henry, say hello to my new friend."

Henry made a few polite comments and with reference to Robert's abilities in any situation made his exit.

Robert poured himself another glass of sherry commenting on my trip. He elaborated on mud turtles, who as mothers leave their young unattended without a backward glance.

I defended myself. "I'm not married anymore. Marriage is merely a string of socially-cemented, stale days. All criticism, love, and indifference are provided by a one-member human race. John wouldn't let me work or go back to school. I handled the children's emergencies, paid the bills with his money, and he ruled. I thought I could sit quietly rocking. Waiting to be a grandmother seemed feasible. Nancy's children need me alive—at least somewhere."

Robert was mumbling when he told me the story of his brother's successful suicide during The Great Depression when he found he couldn't attend college. At least temporarily they agreed life was worth living as best one could. Robert took my hand and asked when I would return to Jackson, Michigan.

* * *

May 27, 1969
Bibliopole, Jackson, Michigan

Robert turned toward the doorway as he heard me lightly running up the steps. My footsteps stopped in the hall as I stopped to read Robert's latest bulletins. I wore my hair short in a halo of brown curls.

Henry, seated at an antique desk, turned to notice then pretended to concentrate on the stack of books before him.

Robert addressed me, "I remember you—Somerset Maugham collector, selling books on bicycles. I thought you were on the lam from your kids."

"That's me," I said. "Was it Ambrose Bierce that claimed Maugham stole his only real woman character, Rosie of *Cakes and Ale* right out of Anatole France's *Under the Rose?"* I dropped my purse next to a chair and offered my hand to Robert.

"It was the author of *The Devil's Dictionary,* a plagiarism suit. And that would have been Bierce."

"I'm collecting first editions of Anatole France now—and anything about Gauguin. Well that is after I get a job. I had to run again. John followed Nancy to Illinois, so I left."

Without speaking, Henry filled his pen out of Robert's inkstand. He listed the costs of the books, opening each cover and writing down the price on the tablet. He efficiently found his calculator, wrote out a check, and placed it in the middle of Robert's desk.

Henry left with the books, came back, setting the books down to put on his coat. He exited with the books only to come back, setting the books down again to tug on his gloves, leaving without the books. His shoes were brown and terribly scuffed. One pant leg had its hem torn out so it dragged over the shoe. The other pant leg was too short and revealed a bright yellow sock above the shabby shoe with its laces trailing.

* * *

ANOTHER MAY 1969 VISIT
BIBLIOPOLE, JACKSON, MICHIGAN

The late afternoon lit the bookshop. Three domed windows turned rosy and then darkened enough for the desk lamp and one wall light to be switched on. Dark wood bookcases and a high back drop-leaf desk interspersed the eight-foot windows. "Bibliopole" was printed in reverse on the window nearest Robert's desk. The rear wall had a low row of bookshelves with two framed oil paintings centered above them. All the walls of the shop were lined with bookshelves and a set of free standing shelves divided the rear of the shop into two walkways. The front area was the same width as the rear except for the doorway. The door was blocked open with a large fossil. Robert's cluttered desk set diagonally faced the entrance. Two smaller bookcases framed a closed door to the bookman's quarters. Five unmatched chairs and many boxes filled with books completed the scene.

Henry, about the same age (fifty-two) but thicker and slightly balding, was seated at the drop-leaf bookcase. During conversations he rarely spoke but methodically searched his brown wool suit coat for his checkbook, going through the pockets of his camel hair overcoat that was carefully folded on the back of a chair. He fished the same for his ink pen, which was in his shirt pocket, under a tan sweater vest. He unscrewed the fountain pen and tried it on a tablet on the table.

"You're back?" Robert seemed delighted to see me again.

"I'm a fellow citizen," I said.

"Anti-social witchlet. How are Nancy's babies?"

"She doesn't know what to do. John's overwhelming and spying on her. He was always there when she visited the boys, in a threatening distrustful way. I just want to think."

"Essential for every day."

"My own thoughts."

"You're the only one you must answer. Glass of sherry?" Robert pulled out a desk drawer, found a bottle of sherry and small glasses.

"Fine, what is it?"

"It's for my friends, and generally from my friends."

I sat in the chair closest to Robert, sighed and crossed my legs to reveal quite a bit of thigh. I sipped the sweet sherry, noticed my dress and tugged at it unsuccessfully.

Since the owner's name was in each book Robert explained to Henry how he had acquired his latest cache of books. "Seems this tennis pro in town was caught teaching more than a backstroke. The injured wife took up smoking to alleviate her drinking problem and a match somehow got flicked into the wastepaper basket in her husband's study. The trophies are undamaged, but the fire flashed quickly and melted everything plastic in the house. The books," Robert coughed the lie, "were in the basement so the smell of smoke was their only legacy. Apparently she has quite a collection. She hustled me out after I assured her the books were undamaged. She did let me have a few on consignment with a promise of more if they sell."

Henry left without the books he had purchased, even dropping one glove, which he retrieved, bringing further attention to his disgraceful shoes.

"Were you ever married?" I asked after he departed.

"Once." Robert frowned.

"Sounds final. Another man?"

"Yes. Her father." Robert poured himself another glass of sherry. He shook himself, refilled my glass and patted my shoulder. "I was sued for non-support."

"I'm going to be okay," I said.

"I can see that. I just worry about Nancy's children."

"I'm sure they know they're loved."

"That's not what they'll be told."

I took Robert's hand and promised to come again.

Robert grabbed a book off his desk, shut off the lights,

opened the door to his quarters, turned on a light inside and said, "Good evening, Miss Poi."

His cat responded.

* * *

JUNE, 1969
WATERLOO, MICHIGAN

The Bibliopole was a unique haven, where customers and friends were allowed to drop the strictures and defensive pretenses of the street-level existence. They ascended up one flight into the soul of humanity to find themselves alive and well. History and constant loving souls lined the shelves.

The air was thick with ideas and freedom. Bare board floors and sun-touched walls suggested an afternoon confessional, but no penances were meted out except love and understanding. Dimly lit, warm-voiced evenings summoned visions of scheming opium dens but innocent conversation was the only drug. They were all lovers, the platonic breed, sharing their inner selves without fear of rejection. Because of this freedom from conformity, Robert's friends were a bit unusual. They looked to him to sing the song of their hearts and kindle the flame in their eyes—to spice life for them.

Henry's family ran a cleaning establishment in town. He was a successful head of the business and an accomplished artist of no fame—perhaps because he artistically followed three rabbit paths at once. He married a woman whom Robert called Lady Macbeth's mad sister. Sara was given a frightening description of tyrannical and oppressive behavior. Their daughter was closeted from any unnecessary contact with the world. Robert remembered lunching with them when she was still a child. The mother made her don white gloves to use the public restroom. When the girl was eighteen, her mother drove her around the outside of the football stadium to hear the homecoming crowd's cheers. She wasn't allowed to attend.

Pete was not an intellectual but responsive and skillful as well as appreciative of beauty. He collected ancient ivories and cloisonné. He flew model airplanes and was an expert photographer. Divorced, the family hearth had been so ingrained with hate that his spouse and daughter taught his dog to bark and growl at him.

Ed had met Robert through his father, one of Robert's teachers. Ed and his German wife lived in Ann Arbor a stone's throw from Nancy's house. I had seen the couple strolling arm in arm one spring evening while I stood at my picture window. Ed's passion for life lightly bubbled in his soul. A mere flick of conversation or warming liquor could boil this handsome kettle to a delightful stir. When he was excited his dark eyes were pinpoints demanding attention. His body flexed with each spirited word. He was a lovely, splendid human.

There were others. When invited to dine with one disarming couple in Waterloo, I was cautioned to watch out if either of them was driving. They didn't use their driveway but drove all over the yard, hitting each other's cars, even slamming into the house—witnessed by gaping holes in the wood siding. While we were talking to the hostess, the host entered the yard driving a tractor at least thirty miles an hour. He barreled into the yard next to the house, surely not a foot away, peeping in the windows as he rumbled by.

When he'd showered and presented himself, I boldly commented on his unusual attire—all bright yellow-green shades, even his shoes. He disappeared without a word, re-entering ten minutes later in purple—shoes and all.

The hostess was not exactly normal company either. She kept bragging that she could make the best gravy anyone ever tasted. She did too. They had a fleet of dachshunds that painfully bit the couple whenever they chose. I felt as if I'd entered Alice's land of wonder.

Joe Wilcox was a lawyer known as Jumping Joe. When excited, no matter how dignified the place, he would jump up about three feet and come down in the same spot. He was short and rounded, every ounce energy. Robert described him as a slightly demented teddy bear. Joe often let Robert and me use his mansion for weekends of madcap, hatter-inspired insanities.

* * *

August, 1969
Two story Condo
Hoffman Estates, Illinois

I arranged for Robert to write me in care of a box number in Plato Center, a town sixty miles away. On the way home from work in Elgin, I would bury his letters in a deserted graveyard. I doubted whether I would have survived a week without this deception.

Robert wrote back, "O dearest of Brattlings?, O Most Zapiferous of Witchlets!, O Most beloved of Hooligans! You can imagine what Nick said when he opened the mail this morning: 'Hey, what the fuck's all this about? Somebody gotta be crazy. You think maybe this place Colonel Saunders or Tom McAn? I tell you once I tell you a hunner'd times—we gotta get some god damn organization around this place.'"

"I didn't know what to do Sunday. I tried filing my heels, but in a way that only we could understand, but that reminded me of you. When I went to get something to eat,

I saw some green tomato pickles which you should have eaten. Miss Poi, too, was uneasy about your absence and has made inquiries about her little cousin Sweets. I looked in my closet and found a white poplin jacket with brass buttons and some leaves in the pocket. I wandered about for a while and came down to the shop. Stuart and Mary, seeing the window open, stopped in and asked me to go to Lum's with them, which I did. Everybody you met asks about you and I've told several people you entered a nunnery in Pratt Falls, Minnesota, which is training go-go sisters to serve mass.

"My aimlessness of the past week has been somewhat refocused by the arrival yesterday of my dear friend, Connor, who would have been delighted with you. He will be here for about ten days and we always find delightful things to do, which I wish you could have shared with us. Connor brought me two excellent Paleozoic fossils, one of which is large enough to serve as a doorstop for the Bibliopole. It is the oldest thing I have around here, being approximately four hundred million years of age, and thus my senior by several weeks. This was a period before God or somebody like that took over—I love you. P.S. I like to think of you finding consolation in being with Nancy's boys, and hope that Johnny is good to you."

Later, another letter came from him:

"Dear, I have just heard your voice on the telephone. Unfortunately, there were people in the shop, but I simply could not cut you off with the *Hatter* code. I am, in fact, most distracted in trying to write this letter to you. Henry and all three Connors are in and out of here, making it impossible for me to continue if I would get this in the Wednesday mail. I shall therefore wrap this up and write you again tomorrow. You are very dear to me, my dear. Know that I love you and that you are always in my thoughts and my heart."

I wrote back, "There is some harsh dame walking these halls who insists she'll love no one but you. How ridiculous! Everyone knows love comes from the will, not up from the unconscious. It is no ungovernable emotion. Why can't she see how reasonable it is to love conventionally? I really must speak to the girl."

* * *

My boss had helped weather the storm of the custody suit. After the divorce I took a note into his office to explain without breaking down. "Newton saw an apple fall and discovered the Law of Gravity. Eve made an apple fall and discovered the Gravity of Law," Alexander King, *Evocations of Love.*"

Half-hour later, my boss handed me his poem as an answer.

"An impetuous lass was Eve
Her innocence t'would be naïve to believe!
She spotted that fruit,
Snapped Mankind a salute –
And with a heave through the trees
Reaped Adam's sheaves
Leaving naught
But a sigh
For
Reprieve."

Robert continued to write me, "Darling, Saturday afternoon I had completed a letter to you and laid it on my desk when along came a wind and rainstorm and snatched up the letter, along with my *tripewriter* cover, and flung both of them in the general direction of Orange Street. The cover I replaced this morning, but I fear the letter is lost forevermore to posterity, and the grief of my future biographers can be but dimly imagined. Now then! Connor left and Henry came, bearing with him another nesuke which he bought yesterday. I did not allow Henry to depart empty-handed. While he was here a fine praying mantis appeared upon my window. Loath to see it squashed in traffic, or starved to death, I captured him and turned him over to Henry, who will transport him to the Essex Heights woods, where he will doubtless prey for gnats, mosquitoes, and other insects less pious than himself, much as the Reverend Alice Katz goes to the cellar and preys for mice. Stuart and Mary were here Saturday and there appears to be some visible evidence that Mary may be bearing twin pachyderms, or at least Gog and Magog. The issue should be quite interesting if she can avoid being trampled to death from the inside.

"Did you leave a bracelet at Lum's? I cannot divert my attention from the absent witchlet to see people or do things, and don't really want to. Your absence becomes almost as palpable as your presence and fills the whole day to the exclusion of anything else. It seems unnatural that your voice and touch are not here with me. I just don't understand Sundays anymore. Shall I see if the Baptists can explain it to me?"

* * *

In the mirrors held up to me in the bookshop, my faults of selfishness, vanity, and the motivation to justify any satisfaction were unavoidable. Running away had just left problems on hold, waiting like so many dirty dishes. The safest subject will always be books. I think I substituted books for friends. They never change and sit patiently on the shelves at my beck and call. They are never too busy to offer a word of advice or comfort. I might have become a librarian but I thought they were like nuns, priestesses of mysteries, unable to have sex or children. I couldn't live if I couldn't read. Sometimes knowing other humans suffer lightens the burden.

EPILOGUE

January 29, 1972
Schaumburg, Illinois

ON MY OLDEST SON'S BIRTHDAY, still married to my second husband, I returned to my sons' home. My first attempt to write down the reasons for leaving was called Digesting Others. I read the book out loud to their father in one sitting. I never fathomed his feelings nor discerned his motives. I wanted him to understand how I had developed during the nine years of our marriage when we had become strangers to each other—as well as the twenty-seven months I was without my children.

I used a lot of quotes and footnoted philosophy in this first try. Maybe the Bibliopole was the only fit place for quotes. He did weep; promising if we ever broke up the children would be mine. I knew he would never have another day of peace now that I had secured the children. He left us the day after Christmas that year. I was awarded legal custody of my children before I divorced my second husband.

The second reading of Digesting Others was by an editor of a Texas newspaper who was visiting his sister in Elgin, Illinois. At the time men, mostly married men, were crawling in through the windows and doors. I think I wore an available-victim hat, but I'd become accustomed to attention. Between his editorial comments, he fell in love with me. I hated every mark he put on the page and it crossed my mind that the 'I love you' statements were just to placate me. But he ended the project by asking me to marry him. He smoked and coughed, his skin was nearly yellow, and he didn't have a job. I'd been raising my two sons for three years.

I couldn't see taking care of a grown man—editor or not. So I told him no. And then, he wouldn't speak to me. At the time it seemed crazy. How could a person want to marry you one minute and not want to even speak to you the next?

As to the fictitious encounters referred to in the above pages, a lot of unbeautiful people have a lot of unforgettable romances and sexual exploits, so none of this is noteworthy—just bizarre to those involved. If we had the time or inclination to breach each other's privacy, we would find our own marathons of sex or agonies of unrequited love were common as grass, and guilt is ridiculous. Only at times does commitment help to make some act, some affection, meaningful.

Nevertheless, the first attempt, Digesting Others, regained custody of my two children and a marriage proposal.

* * *

March 1, 1990
Ann Arbor, Michigan

When my sons were both in their fifties, I returned to visit the Ann Arbor house where I had lived when I left their father. I imagined roaming the empty rooms for four years—

from 1965 to 1969. My soul had left that homemaker, hovering over the aimless wandering carcass. The mighty oak of over 200 years was gone except for a stump about three feet in diameter. Had my requested blue roses felled the oak? I know the Lord loves me enough to convince me I am forgiven.

Made in the USA
Middletown, DE
11 April 2023